although our [...]
hard at times ... it is worth
the trip.

[signature]

ALONE
IN THE
DARKNESS

IN SEARCH OF HOPE

ALONE
IN THE
DARKNESS

IN SEARCH OF HOPE

A TRUE STORY OF LIFE, DEATH AND SPIRITUALITY ON EARTH AND BEYOND

BY
VALERIE DZIENGIEL

MILL CITY PRESS

Mill City Press, Inc.
2301 Lucien Way #415
Maitland, FL 32751
407.339.4217
www.millcitypress.net

Printed in the United States of America

ISBN-13: 978-1-54565-013-4

Table of Contents

Dedications

My story is dedicated to my sister, Lydia and
her husband, Tom;
my daughter, Jennifer and her husband, Tom;
my nieces, Marianne and Caroline;
and a very special friend, Renee;
who made notable attempts to reach out to me
during my loss and grieving;
and especially to God,
who inspired the words embraced upon these pages.

Acknowledgement: Special thanks to my sister, Lydia and
my brother-in-law, Tom. They both spent years reading and
re-reading my story, suggesting improvements to enhance
its appeal.

Introduction

How many times have we heard the question, What is the meaning of life? In response, my query would be: When we were born did we start life with a blank manuscript or have the opportunities we have been presented, which fill infinite pages, been eloquently written prior to our birth?

None of us know for sure. So, given a choice, my belief is that the achievement of the completion of a soul's journey through the positive and negative events we are meant to encounter, is the reason for life itself. Therefore, I have faith that God, in His Almighty Wisdom, provides us with a life of constant change through various predetermined trials we are meant to endure to fulfill the purpose of our life's journey.

Because we have free will, we may either conquer or succumb to these challenges; but in the end, the quality of our existence may depend upon our willingness to travel difficult paths we would prefer to avoid.

When faced with adversity, my faith in God helped me learn from my life's lessons, grow stronger from the experience, and pass on the wisdom I gained for the benefit of others.

Each day is a new beginning, and the journey we take is intended to improve our life as a result of our experiences, both good and bad. We need to learn how to overcome destructive forces we encounter, for we all have the ability to remake our lives after catastrophe. More important than the tribulations which test us during our life, are our reactions to these events and how we handle their consequences. It is the end result, that is to say, how we finish the course we travel, which counts the most.

Keep in mind, my journey through life has not been perfect. It is not a Cinderella story. There is no such thing as a perfect life. One does not come to this realm to experience Utopia . . . for if this is your hope, you will definitely be disappointed.

As a result of spiritual paranormal events which occurred shortly after my husband's death, I was driven, compelled is perhaps a better description, to share my story. Even though sadness and grief were my constant companion during his illness and after his death, I strongly believe there was an intended purpose to my anguish. Throughout my ordeal, I learned how to cope with adversity, muster enough strength to get on with my life, and follow through with the inspiration I attained, in order to help others by writing my memoir.

There are many reasons why the survivor is meant to live on. I believe my continued existence enabled me to share the knowledge that grief can be overcome. If you find the right formula which works for you, you won't have to live the remainder of your life feeling empty and sad. It just takes time.

My story describes the path I traveled, and how my prayers, convictions, intuition, and belief in God guided me through life, enabling me to experience its joys and sadness.

When you read some of my thought-provoking phrases, I have faith they originated from beyond my awareness. Sometimes, I was unable to write fast enough to capture the ideas flowing through my mind. Many a night, I arose from my warm bed to seize these thoughts and avoid forgetting their inspiration before dawn.

I could not summon the words to come. They drifted, as if on a ocean breeze, and culminated into passages of inspiration I myself found mystical.

Although my journey has been more difficult alone, the hardships I encountered have made me better appreciate the adventure called life, since every obstacle we face is meant to be confronted, even if it cannot be conquered.

There will be no names in my story, just pronouns. We are all husbands, wives, mothers, fathers, sisters, brothers, children, aunts, uncles, nieces, nephews and friends. Therefore, feel free to substitute the names you feel are appropriate, in order to bring my story into your heart.

CHAPTER 1

A Life of Constant Change

In the beginning . . . how Biblical a place to start . . . my life began as the middle child of parents who grew up during the Great Depression in Brooklyn and New York City.

Mom and Dad met at a Polish Club social. Eventually, they fell in love and married toward the end of WW II, after Dad's Honorable Discharge from the U.S. Army-Air Force. Eventually, three children completed the family picture.

My brother is the oldest, and I came in second place, by a matter of a whole three minutes, because my sister and I are twins. In our early childhood, I boasted the position of being the older sister. As time went on, my sister never let me forget this distinction.

Our family called Brooklyn home, once Dad changed work positions after a short stint as a woodworker in a local factory in New York City. My father became gainfully employed at the Brooklyn Navy Yard because my maternal grandfather encouraged this change. Grandpa believed a government position would provide better job security for our family. After all, Grandpa knew firsthand how difficult hard times could be, especially since he raised his family through the grim times of the Depression while my mother was in her childhood. As it turned out, this change was a good move for all of us.

During my elementary school years, my sister and I attended St. Michael's Catholic Grammar School, and our religious instruction became the basis for most of my life's beliefs.

My father, who loved the outdoors, didn't want to raise his family in the city. He was thrilled when the Brooklyn Navy Yard closed, and he was afforded the opportunity to move out of state.

It was a blessing for us all. If it weren't for this life-altering event, our family might never have left New York and moved to Connecticut . . . and I, quite possibly, might never have met my husband.

When I was a teenager, my choice for a husband was idyllic, and there wasn't a long list of boyfriends in my life. Starting at a young age, my compatibility requirements far outweighed my desire to stay in a relationship, just so I wouldn't be alone. In order for me to continue to date a young man, there had to be a special connection. The longevity of my involvements were usually very short. If it didn't feel right, I would quickly end a relationship because I wanted to be available when the right person came along. By the ripe old age of sixteen, my friends in Brooklyn determined I would marry the first young man who could last in a relationship with me for longer than a two week period. Although this statement was not 100% accurate, it was very close to the truth.

Six months had passed since our move from NY, and my life hadn't turned out to be the romantic adventure I had hoped for. At that time, I often wondered, would I ever meet the love of my life?

The *Sound of Music* had recently been the number one movie on the big screen. Like Liesl, I was also sixteen, going on seventeen, with fanciful dreams of finding true love.

A big change would soon take place in my life because I was about to meet my future husband for the first time. Although it wasn't love at first sight, it was darn close to it.

It was early spring in 1966, and I had driven some of my girlfriends to Norwich, CT to a local teenage hangout called Friendly's. It was a new adventure for me because this was

2

the first time I had gone there. Our mission was to meet boys, but the anticipation of the event fizzled when there were none to be found.

Since I had just recently earned my driver's license and it was getting late, I suggested to my friends that it was time we started to head home. I didn't want to run into trouble finding my way in the dark on the unfamiliar roads.

What happened next was unexpected. As I prepared to start the car, a young man with a confident stride, slowly approached us. Once he reached the opposite side of my car, he boldly asked for a kiss from all the girls present because he claimed it was his birthday. I watched in amazement as each girl eagerly responded to his charms.

When he finally reached my open driver's window, in reply to his attempted bold advances I said, "I don't know you, and I won't kiss you!"

Although he had already received some endearing kisses from all the other girls who were present, he was unhappy with my refusal.

I must have hurt his ego because he then walked to the front of my car, opened the hood and disconnected the distributor cap. Once he returned to my window, he said he wouldn't fix my car until I kissed him.

Now that I couldn't start the car and had no idea how to repair it myself, I pleaded with him, stating, "If I don't meet my curfew, I will be disciplined when I got home."

He then crouched down next to me with his chin resting upon his hands as he held onto the bottom portion of the window frame. I was intimidated by his boldness when he leaned forward and whispered into my ear, "All you have to do is kiss me and I will fix your car."

As he spoke, his lips were close to mine while he waited with anticipation for me to turn my head to receive his kiss.

Embarrassed by the situation I was in, instead of looking directly at him, I stared at the opened car hood while I tried to determine what I should do.

I now realized it was up to me to make the next move. So, I turned my body toward him and placed my fingertips on his chin. As I gently turned his face to the left, I placed a quick kiss upon his cheek.

Apparently, I caught him off guard because at that point, as promised, he stood up and walked to the front of the car. While his face was hidden from my view, he fixed the problem he had caused and closed the hood.

Because it was getting darker, I quickly started the car and put the standard shift into gear. Driving out of the otherwise deserted parking lot, I looked in my rearview mirror and saw him standing all alone, but I couldn't make out his face as he watched me drive away.

A few days later, I returned to Friendly's alone. While I sat at the breakfast bar counter daydreaming and sipping a cup of coffee, a male voice interrupted my thoughts.

Startled, I looked up to see a tall, slender, dark-haired young man. As he started to sit down in the seat right next to me, he asked, "Can I buy you another cup of coffee?"

At first, I didn't realize he was the same young man who wanted *the kiss* a few nights earlier. That night, in the twilight hours, I had only seen his obscured face for a minute or two and I didn't make the connection when he spoke to me.

Something about his confidence was extremely appealing, and I smiled when I accepted his invitation. I could tell from the start, he was older and more mature than me. Nonetheless, we quickly settled into a comfortable conversation. Within a short period of time, I felt as though we had known each other forever.

Of course, at this particular moment, neither one of us had any idea how dramatically our lives would change as a result of our meeting that night.

It wasn't long before he knew my whole life's story, since I quickly explained the events which resulted in my recent move from New York to Connecticut.

In turn, he told me that he lived with his parents in Norwich. Among other things, he talked about the type of work he had done for his brother, who was in the excavation business.

Our friendship blossomed further over our numerous coffee conversations. Each time he saw me, he made a point to come over to talk to me since we got along so well. However, despite our compatibility, I didn't entertain the idea of a romantic relationship with him. After all, he was nineteen, and I thought he was too old for me.

Apparently, he had other ideas. To my surprise, within a few weeks after we first met he asked me out on a date, and I accepted.

From that day forward, he always referred to *that kiss*, as the cheap kiss which started our relationship. As our romance blossomed, he told me he searched me out because I refused to kiss him when we first met.

After our relationship developed, there were many times when he would mention how much he wanted to meet me again after our first encounter. A smile comes to my face as I write these words . . . for I, too, never forgot that day!

CHAPTER 2

Love Blossoms

Spring was in full bloom, and our first date was a new experience for me. When he came to pick me up, I had no idea where we were going. For that matter, I didn't really care.

As we drove along, curiosity got the best of me. So, when I asked where we were headed, he answered, "To the drive-in."

Although he was relaxed, I was nervous, and sat way over to the right side of the front seat of his pick-up truck. When he asked if I planned to sit that far from him all night, somewhat intimidated, I moved closer.

After we arrived at the drive-in and he parked the truck, he then wanted to know if I intended to keep my coat on all night. When I told him I was cold, he said he would keep me warm.

Once the movie started, I reluctantly took off my coat and before I could object, his arm was around me and we kissed. My immediate reaction was that I didn't want him to stop kissing me. I had never felt that way before about any other guy. It was tender and exciting, all in one. To this day, I couldn't tell you the name of the movie we went to, but I never forgot his kiss!

In 1964, Betty Everett's #1 Hit, the Shoop, Shoop Song, a/k/a *It's In His Kiss,* became one of my favorite tunes because that was exactly how I felt. He was a handful and had pushed the boundaries, but he respected the limits I set, and before I knew it, the night was over.

As he drove me home, I wondered if this would be my first and last date, while at the same time, he deliberated whether or not he should ask me out again.

Later in our relationship, he told me he wasn't sure if I would accept, especially after the hard time he had given me that night.

Of course, as that evening was drawing to a close, I wanted him to ask me out on a second date but wasn't sure he was interested in me. It was obvious he was used to getting his way, and that wasn't the kind of person I was.

Even though we talked on the way home, he didn't mention a second date until he reached my driveway and pulled in. My heart jumped for joy when he asked if I would like to go out with him the following weekend. Of course, I said yes.

For the first time in my life, I felt that special feeling I had been searching for. We were extremely compatible, and there were sparks too!

In that short period of time since our initial meeting, it felt like I had known him my whole life, and our first date led to our dating every weekend thereafter.

Obviously, we were falling in love. We both sensed something special had developed as a result of our initial encounter. Fortunately, he felt the same way I did, about finding his perfect match. He, too, was searching for the girl he hoped would make him complete . . . the one he would marry.

Within a very short period of time, the intensity of our commitment to each other became undeniable. Yes, I knew he was the one!

There were always many interested females from which he could choose; he was just that kind of guy. He was exciting and manly, but most importantly, he was an extremely caring individual.

As our love blossomed, our conversation often revisited our first meeting, which led to our first date. I loved asking him why he picked me, and he enjoyed kidding me in return, and would always say, "Although you are not the prettiest girl I've ever dated, you are a clean-cut kid." He always made sure to add, it was because "There is something special about you." Maybe not a title some girls would strive for, but it was a compliment to me.

Even though he was experienced, he acknowledged, if I were any other way, our relationship wouldn't have lasted.

Two and a half months passed quickly. It was now Memorial Day Weekend and we were at our favorite hangout spot on Ocean Beach, near the concession stand.

While lying down on our beach blanket, my sweetheart's leg was bent in an arched manner, so as to enable me to lean against it. This allowed us to face each other as we carried on our conversation. As I longingly gazed into his eyes, he captivatingly inquired, "If I asked you to marry me . . . what would you say?"

I was shocked! Up until now, we were only dating. At this point, in our short relationship, I only hoped he would ask me to go steady. Instead, he was asking for a real commitment. It was not what I expected to hear.

My brain was in a whirlwind. I thought . . . married? I was only sixteen and wouldn't be seventeen for six more weeks. I was just a kid!

Of course, in that day and age, many of my friends would be married upon graduation, right after they turned eighteen. Therefore, during this time period, his intention to establish a commitment was the norm.

Still, I wondered why he asked this question now . . . because it took me by complete surprise. I thought it was so unlike him. So many thoughts ran through my mind as I wondered if I was ready to make such a pledge. Nevertheless, I knew my answer would be a life changer.

In retrospect, we were already spending all of our free time together. My thoughts quickly turned to how special our relationship had become and how much I loved him.

Since honesty in a relationship was so important to me, before I would answer, I had to think it through.

Although in my mind it seemed like an eternity, it only took seconds before I told him, "I would say yes!"

Actually, I knew he wasn't really asking me to marry him. I understood from the question, by the way it was phrased, "If I asked you . . .," it was just a supposition.

What he really wanted to know was whether or not I cared for him as much as he cared for me.

There was no question, the feeling was mutual.

Soon, I realized the reason for his question ran deeper than his desire to know where he stood in our relationship. Up until now, my thoughts centered around how happy we were together and where we would go on our next date, while he was planning our future together.

Quite unexpectedly, the next words out of his mouth were, "Will you wait for me?" I innocently replied, "What do you want me to wait for?"

Prior to that moment, he never told me he was headed to Vietnam. For that matter, I didn't even know he was in the service.

Since he lived at home and I never saw him in his uniform, I just assumed he worked for his brother in the construction business. It turned out he had, but only during the period before his active duty service began.

Being so young, I had no interest in watching the news on TV; therefore, I wasn't aware the war in Vietnam was underway.

However, at the moment, all those details no longer mattered. My answer was a quick and easy one to make. In response to his request, I assuredly replied, "Of course I will wait for you. I will wait for you forever, if you want me to."

CHAPTER 3

The Waiting Period

O n that sunny Memorial Day at the beach, my sweetheart had put a path into motion which solidified our budding relationship of young love into a lasting relationship of true love.

Even though we didn't get engaged, I did get his high school ring. He had never given it to anyone before, and I cherished it!

Had it not been for his service obligation, the speed at which our commitment developed would probably have taken a much slower pace. Initially, I didn't understand why the question of marriage arose so quickly. I could easily tell he wasn't the kind of guy to rush into such an important decision as this. He deliberated every move he made and didn't jump into a situation unprepared. So, once I learned he would be serving in Vietnam, the reason became very clear to me.

He told me he had been searching for the right girl for some time. Like me, he never remained in a relationship for long . . . but this time it was different. We both felt a special bond unlike anything we had ever experienced before. One thing was for certain, I knew I had fallen deeply in love.

Family values were very important to him. He appreciated how quickly my parents had accepted him into my family, and I felt the same way about his parents' affection towards me.

Every day was a new adventure. As our love grew stronger, neither of us could ever have imagined how painful our separation would be. A mere four weeks remained until his departure.

Before we knew it, June 30th had arrived. As I watched his plane lift off the tarmac at the Hartford Airport, my heart broke. Although I had accompanied his parents and brother to his sendoff, never had I felt so lonely as I did at that moment. Finally, I had found my soulmate, and he had been taken away from me.

We were not able to celebrate our birthdays or Christmas together that year while I waited faithfully for his return, constantly worrying about the life and death scenario which played out precariously on the other side of the world. During this time, I felt I had matured far beyond my current age of seventeen.

Most girls my age were unaware of the sad uncertainties I agonized over daily, praying he would come home safely, while having no control over the events that shaped our lives. I believed our future was in God's Hands, and I prayed that He would protect him.

Early in our relationship, during his first tour of duty, a cousin of mine recommended that I should not be sitting home alone waiting for him. She felt I should be out dating other guys.

She was two years older than me and thought she was much wiser. She believed that I was too young to be tied down at such a young age. She told me, "You should be out having fun before you settle down."

In reply, I explained that although I was young, I had found something special. This was the relationship I had been searching for. Why would I continue to search for what I had already found?

Time passed slowly until he finally came home during the second semester of my senior year. Sadly, our time together was too short, and our reunion was not permanent.

He was temporarily transferred to Camp Lejeune in South Carolina, for additional training, which included mine and demolition certification. He barely made it home in time for my graduation when he informed me he would soon be redeployed to Vietnam.

This earth-shattering news was like a horrible nightmare. Initially, we were both under the impression he was home for good, but, that was not the case. Now, after recently returning from Camp Lejeune, within six short weeks he would be leaving for Vietnam again. At this point in our relationship, we had spent considerably more time apart than we had together.

His second deployment was worse than the first one, because this time, he knew what he would face when he arrived back in Vietnam. He told me, the only thing that made his military service bearable was the fact I would be waiting for him when he returned home.

While overseas, he served in the northern province of the Da Nang area of Vietnam, near the DMZ, during portions of 1966 and 1967. His second tour took place during the escalation period of the North Vietnamese Army against our troops. Although he never told me much about the war, he did tell me things were heating up quickly, and he was looking forward to coming home.

A high concentration of Agent Orange had been spread over the Vietnamese countryside in the area where he served during this time period, which affected not only the enemy but also our own U.S. armed forces.

Almost two years had passed since our relationship began, and the time finally arrived for his safe return home. As I stood alongside his brother and father, waiting for his plane at the landing field, I could barely wait to be in his arms again.

We were given an estimated time of arrival for an early morning landing, but after a substantial amount of time had passed, we were told the plane was delayed. When his brother inquired as to the reason, he was told engine trouble had caused the plane to experience a forced landing along the way.

Following hours of waiting and worrying, the suspense of this delay was alarming. I can still recall the secrecy of the event at the base where he was due to land. The military airport security was not forthcoming with any details about the actual cause of his late arrival. All I knew was that our joyous reunion wouldn't take place until early afternoon. It wasn't until the ride home that we all learned about the frightening event which caused his delay, when he described the loud troublesome sounds which resulted in one of the plane's engines catching fire and shutting down. He explained how the racket of the engine failure pulsated throughout the inside of the plane. Since there were no windows in the USAF C-141 aircraft, the pilot announced the engine difficulty and stated everything would be fine, pointing out the plane had no problem running on the three remaining engines.

When a second engine malfunctioned shortly after the first one, the familiar sounds of engine failure resonated throughout the plane, but this time there was no encouraging announcement made to settle the nerves of the brave young men inside.

Although the plane now had just two working engines, it was fortunate there was one operational engine on each wing, or else the crew and servicemen on board might not have made it home at all that day. Upon their emergency landing, when he saw both fire-damaged engines, he realized they most likely would have ditched into the vast ocean, miles away from civilization, had the engines been located on the same sides of the plane. It amazed me to hear how calmly he spoke about the second engine failure. He later admitted, he thought he was going to die as a result of the plane crashing after having lived through hell in Vietnam not just once, but twice, as he put it. By the way he spoke, he gave me the impression death was no longer the demon in the night. Now, it was just a reality of life.

Though God had brought him home to me, I later realized he was not unscathed by his participation in the war. Vietnam had changed the young man I met a few years earlier. It matured him into a man who would love and protect me for the rest of his life. Unfortunately, his exposure to Agent Orange resulted in a slow progression of medical maladies which slowly ate away at his core . . . until one day, it finally took his life, and mine too, as a result of his loss.

CHAPTER 4

Good Times Outweighed the Bad

After all the time we had spent apart, we would finally be able to develop our relationship on a truly personal level, instead of by phone or written communication. In a way our love was unique because it had grown from our faith and trust in each other, which, undeniably, had created a very strong foundation for us to build upon.

Because we had no money, we didn't marry immediately after his discharge from the service. He wanted to be able to take care of me, and he was fully aware he wasn't financially able to do so at this point in his life.

We did, however, get engaged the following Christmas once he had a steady job and could afford a ring. After he placed the engagement ring on my finger, he said he had picked it out a while ago but felt it wasn't his to give until he had paid for it.

Many of our friends were married or were already planning to do so. While we spent our time apart, they had already enjoyed their dating and getting to know each other period. Now that my love was home permanently, we needed time to enjoy the activities we had missed out on while we were apart. We went to drive-ins, the beach, took long romantic drives in his convertible and even learned how to water ski. As an added bonus, all of the time we spent together helped us further confirm our compatibility.

Life was full of fun. We really loved our carefree lifestyle with its limited obligations.

Given the fact that the financial responsibility to pay for a wedding of our dreams fell upon our shoulders, we set our wedding date once he felt confident in our fiscal stability. Although I relished the single life we spent together, deep down inside, the anticipation of our marriage was never far from my mind. Now, it was on the horizon.

Our nuptials took place during a tropical depression. Although it poured all morning, the weather couldn't dampen my spirits. My wish had finally come true. I was now married to the love of my life, and I was ecstatic!

At the end of the day's celebration, after we enjoyed the ceremony and reception I had envisioned forever, we walked out of the hall together into the sunlight. As the sun shined brightly upon us, he took me in his arms and we kissed. I smiled when he suggested the storm's clearing was a good omen.

A short time after we returned from our honeymoon, my husband faced an unexpected dilemma at work. Prior to our marriage, in his spare time, he had made extra money flipping older homes. His father was the one who initially suggested he buy a home that needed renovation. Although he wasn't keen on the idea, the investment turned out to be a lucrative venture.

My father and I would help him with painting and cleanup at the end of the day and on the weekends, after all three of us had already put in our eight hours of work each day at our full-time jobs. My husband, who at the time was my fiancé, would also hire subcontractors to work on whatever repair services were beyond his current skills. As a result of his efforts, his endeavor paid off. After this initial success, his profits were invested in subsequent projects. In time, the extra funds made it possible to pay for our dream wedding.

Unfortunately, our lovely nuptial must have made his boss assume my husband devoted too much of his spare time to his outside interests, in order to have been able to afford such an elegant affair. Consequently, my husband was then placed in a position where he had to choose between his current full-time job in advertising or the new entrepreneurship he had recently embraced.

Even though he was taken completely off guard by the ultimatum, my husband found the decision easy to make. Ironically, life seemed to have offered us a golden opportunity when we least expected it.

There was no question, my husband enjoyed the challenge of being a self-made man. He thought running his own business would allow him the ability to control his own destiny while expanding his income potential at the same time. He was a dreamer, and I believed in him.

In fact, as I look back on the choice he had to make, his boss did us a favor. Had it not been for this tribulation, it might have taken a lot longer for us to find our proper path in life, even though, it was a struggle at the time.

Shortly after this life-altering decision was settled, another unanticipated problem arose. It had to do with my health.

Five years earlier, during a medical exam which was a prerequisite for a government position I procured before graduation, I was alerted to the fact that I had irregular heartbeats. At the time, the doctor who examined me led me to believe the condition was not serious, and that I would outgrow the disorder.

Wanting to believe the doctor's opinion that my irregular heartbeats weren't serious, throughout the years I ignored several requests from my gynecologist to seek additional medical advice to determine whether or not I needed some sort of heart treatment.

In time, due to my own stubbornness and aversion for doctors, I developed a severe case of shortness of breath, a side effect of my heart ailment.

Now, recently married and in my early 20's, believing I was too young for something to be seriously wrong with me, I continued to shrug off the possibility of a serious health condition until my gynecologist highly recommended it was time I scheduled an appointment to get my heart condition assessed prior to deciding to have children. I recall her stating, the heart wasn't her specialty, but she felt it was time I obtained an accurate evaluation of my ailment because a pregnancy could put me at risk for potential complications. To say she appeared concerned, was an understatement.

Once I relayed the message to my husband, he no longer accepted my defense that there was nothing to worry about. He insisted I schedule an appointment A.S.A.P. While I was not a fan of doctors, at my husband's request, I finally scheduled an appointment with a doctor of internal medicine, who specialized in the heart. Since I had expected a clean bill of health, I was surprised when the doctor immediately ordered an EKG be performed in his office.

After the test was completed, while I dressed in the examination room, the doctor spoke to my husband, telling him my condition was extremely serious. The EKG results indicated excessive irregular heartbeats, with almost no regular beats amongst them. The doctor voiced his concern, stating my heart wouldn't be able to continue to function under such irregularities, and it was possible that within the next six months I might have a stroke, heart attack, or possibly even die if the condition went untreated.

The doctor cautioned, if no one was available to stay with me 24-hours a day, I would have to be placed in a hospital. Since surgery wasn't an option and the only treatment available was to place me on heart medication, my husband wanted to take care of me at home. My husband thought I would be more comfortable if he looked after me, and the doctor agreed. In case of an emergency, we were given the doctor's home phone number, and in the event emergency care became necessary, the hospital was located a short distance from where we lived.

As forewarned, except for the limited periods of time my husband would wake me to eat the food he had prepared to sustain me, the medication caused me to sleep around the clock.

Within the next two weeks, my heart slowly responded to the medication and started to show signs of some regularity. The doctor finally began to feel confident about my recovery. When he gave us the promising news, his expression of extreme concern, exhibited at my first visit, had softened to a smile.

The update was encouraging, but due to our financial situation, I was afraid of losing my job if I didn't go back to work soon. Unquestionably, I would be paid for two weeks sick leave, however, my salary and our health insurance, our only steady source of income, would stop if I didn't return to work.

Although it was against my husband's wishes, I insisted upon my returning to work because we had no other choice. Since he couldn't disagree with this rationalization, my husband finally accepted my assessment, provided I didn't have any setbacks.

During this period, he was the one who bore all the mental responsibilities of dealing with the possibility of my death at such an early age. In the autumn of our lives together, I would learn how difficult that responsibility would be.

As I slowly recovered, financial difficulties followed. His recent self-employment had thrown us into a new cycle of fiscal responsibility. Because all of his financial goals were based upon two steady paychecks, money now became an issue. Although in time, the house flipping projects provided a good income, they didn't provide a steady weekly salary.

Since we no longer had two fixed incomes, in order to eliminate our car payment, we had to sell the new car he was so proud of. The cupboards were bare and spaghetti became a main staple for us to live on.

Nonetheless, we survived. In time, we learned how to prepare for the good times, as well as the bad. Most importantly, when faced with this type of adversity, we realized how uncertain our time on earth could be, and this knowledge strengthened our bond even more.

It took a while, but within a few years, the doctor thought I had improved to the point where I could stop taking the medication. His final prognosis led us to believe I could live a normal life. On the side of caution, he alleged that my improved irregular heartbeats would become the new normal for me, but he was happy to advise us that the possibility of having children was not out of the question, although it still could be risky.

Eventually, my husband discovered food allergies appeared to have caused some of my problems. His observations of problematic symptoms which arose when I ate certain foods containing monosodium glutamate, high concentrations of sugar or certain seasonings, led my husband to believe these foods ingredients caused allergic reactions which affected my heart. Once I began to eliminate these substances from my diet, my irregular heartbeats decreased. Had my husband not been so attentive, I don't know if I would be alive today.

A few more years passed, and my mother-in-law was dying from breast cancer. Dealing with her mortality made us question if we should have children at this time in our life. Recalling his letters from Vietnam, we had discussed having three children once we were married. Although he never said it, I believed he was too worried about my health to consider having children at all.

Even though I was no longer on medication, my heart would never be normal. From time to time, I could feel its irregularities. My gynecologist had warned us . . . the stress of childbirth could cause a relapse of my heart condition, and she insisted there was no way she could safely predict an outcome. She pointed out, the delivery would be the most crucial part of a pregnancy; and stated, it was up to us to make the important decision as to whether or not we wanted to risk having children.

We decided to take the chance, and I became pregnant right away. Things went well until it was time for our daughter to be born. While on the delivery room table at the hospital, preoccupied with the procedures of having our baby, my husband was fixated on the heart monitor which displayed troubling irregularities. Once the nurse became aware of his concern, she turned the screen, so he could no longer observe my situation.

Fortunately, the delivery didn't turn into an emergency. Nevertheless, just to be sure I didn't run into any unexpected problems, I was kept in the hospital for an extra day.

Even though we were excited to be new parents, due to the risks involved, we decided not to have any more children. My husband didn't want to chance losing me in order to have a larger family.

Almost seven years had passed before we became a family of three. Instead of returning to work after our daughter was born, we decided it was the perfect opportunity for me to leave the security of my job behind. As an alternative, I became my husband's full-time secretary and office manager. Our business had grown too large for him to run the on-site construction management, as well as handle the daily office routine. Since I would be working out of our home, my career change allowed me the opportunity to help my husband while I took care of our daughter as well.

The next three decades were spent building our business, raising our daughter, and struggling through the ups and downs of the economy which always had a direct impact on our business.

It was usually feast or famine. Our ability to learn how to build up our cash reserves, to survive the many recessionary periods we encountered, amazed me. Yet, it was so simple. *Don't spend money you haven't earned yet*! Fortunately, no matter whether it was a good year or one of the many bad ones, we were a team and always supported each other during these difficult times.

Throughout our lives together, he was always in charge, yet considerate of me in ways I knew no other man would ever be. I always appreciated the fact that he valued my opinion when decisions needed to be made, and he considered me to be an asset to the business he developed. In addition to the loving relationship we shared in our marriage, he made me feel important as a person. Many times, he told me I was the only woman he could ever have lived with because he knew he was demanding and set in his ways. On the other hand, I always felt blessed to be the one he chose.

The fact that we were opposites may have been what he found attractive about me. Although he was worldly, I was not. He had a lust for life, whereas I was naive and somewhat apprehensive to travel the difficult path we needed to take in order to be independent and successful in life.

Not being an adventurous soul, I always wanted to play things safe. My husband gave me the courage to experience so many wonderful aspects of our existence together because of his strong influence upon me. I often told him, I came along for the ride of my life as a result of his confidence, imagination and courage.

We enjoyed our lives together because we shared common interests, and we knew we could count on each other's strength during our individual times of weakness.

In exchange for my husband's life, I would have given mine in a minute. The thought of living without him was unbearable. He would get angry at me whenever I said, *I wanted to be the first to die*, because I knew he felt the same way about being the one left behind.

Since God chose him first, I discovered my purpose was to care for him, in his time of need, in the same thoughtful manner he had cared for me throughout our lives together. I couldn't imagine how extremely difficult it would have been for him to travel his final journey alone.

Not a day goes by, when I don't think about all the joys and sadness we were blessed to share together. Our experiences and memories are what make us who we are. These things can never be taken away from us.

For the love of my life, from the bottom of my heart, I conveyed my feelings poetically:

> *When it is time for me to leave this earth,*
> *and my journey is complete.*

I want no tears of sadness shed,
only tears of joy to weep.

Eternal joy is heavenly,
for this I'll have to wait.

But soon it's time, he'll come for me,
and my pain will no longer be.

Two souls as one, will reunite again,
and love eternally.

You can now understand a synopsis of our relationship. The hard part is yet to come. My story continues in the autumn of our lives together.

CHAPTER 5

Answering My Prayers

Until we retired a few years ago, while we ran our own business, my husband and I were always early risers. I would like to say it was the economy that forced our hands when it came time for him to make the choice to stop working, but the truth is, my husband's health was the cause of this difficult decision.

It was easier to say he chose to retire because of the long hours and backbreaking work. What my husband didn't want known was that he was ill and could no longer run the business we so proudly built together. The closing of our business was a hard thing to do, but there simply was no choice.

Prior to his diagnosis, my husband had been plagued with Parkinson's symptoms for many years. Early on, because his symptoms were subtle, we didn't relate them to any particular disease. He always thought the tingling, tripping, stability issues and mental confusion was a normal part of aging. Possibly it was fatigue, due to the strenuous work he performed at the construction sites?

As time passed and his symptoms became more noticeable, during a regular annual visit to the VA, his primary care doctor detected tremors in his hand and leg. After a preliminary examination, his doctor proposed a possible diagnosis of Parkinson's disease and suggested he be seen by a VA neurologist. Eventually, the neurologist confirmed the dreaded verdict. Suddenly, all of his symptoms made sense.

His diagnosis was a *difficult pill to swallow* because he was such a masculine man his whole life. Ironically, as the symptoms advanced in his disorder, the italicized phrase exemplified a life-threatening ailment associated with this disease.

Acceptance of the inevitable didn't come easy. This was not a common cold he was suffering from, and his future prospects were bleak.

Knowing how challenging it would become for him to travel the path which lay ahead, we both agreed to keep his diagnosis a secret . . . for the time being.

In order to learn what to expect, while his symptoms progressed, I privately scrutinized medical information online. I soon discovered that medication helped, but there was no cure, which left many unanswered questions in my mind.

Whenever I discovered new facts, I didn't share them with my husband. I didn't want to increase his anxiety because he wasn't receptive to any of the statistics I tried to offer.

For the first time in my life, I felt he was not the one in control. Now it was up to me to understand the ground rules and make the decisions. He entrusted that responsibility to me. It had become too overwhelming to him. In this aspect, while I planned the steps he took during the advancement of his disease, I worried about his gloomy future.

One thing was certain, he had no doubt that I would be there for him. He was the love of my life, my reason for living . . . he was my soulmate. Even though we knew our lives would never be the same, the strength of our relationship gave him the courage to face the adversity of this terrible disease. After all, happiness still existed because we still had each other.

However, I worried how difficult life might become as his disease advanced. He was my rock, the foundation upon which our lives were built. Only now, his core was showing signs of deterioration.

Although he faced many trials and tribulations during his lifetime, he never backed down from any of them. Admirably, he was the type of person who tackled every challenge head on. This trait was evident, whether it entailed surviving the military actions he and his combat brothers experienced in Vietnam, where death was always a way of life, or how he tackled the uphill battles he faced as a young man in making something of himself in this world.

He was a self-made man who accomplished success the hard way. Now, life dealt him the misfortune of diminishing his ability to enjoy the fruits of his labor in our twilight years together.

Granted, he was disillusioned by his destiny, but eventually, he accepted his fate. He resolved himself to accept the life God set in place for him, and we adapted accordingly.

When the time came to determine what we needed to do next, in preparation for the disabilities which would arise as a result of his illness, we planned for our future. Since he had already begun to experience the effects of freezing in place and falling when he walked, we both felt the icy winter weather in CT would be a hindrance to his mobility. We knew the warm weather in the south would be beneficial in more ways than one, especially, since we both enjoyed the outdoors so much.

For my whole life, he had taken care of me. Now it was my turn to take care of him. My main objective was for my husband to be able to enjoy the remainder of his life. So, in order to accomplish this goal, we decided to sell our home and move south. When we traveled to Florida, to scope out different neighborhoods, we both agreed that we would be able to find a suitable place to live in the Ocala area.

Our plans were set in motion. All we needed to do was sell our home and move, or so we thought.

During this time, I begged God to cure him or at least prevent his disease from escalating to the point where he might become wheelchair bound, for I believed that would totally destroy his spirit.

Who knew my prayers would be answered in the way they were.

CHAPTER 6

Life is Rarely Predictable

T he sun was just beginning to rise over the tree line, and it was barely visible through our bedroom picture window. As it started to creep up the covers, its warmth became apparent when it reached my face and stirred me from my sleep. It was a beautiful morning, like so many mornings recently, because spring was in the air.

Winter had been tough this year. Even though its beauty was striking, the snow fell more often than we preferred. We lived deep in the woods, and each snowfall created a winter wonderland around us when the shimmering snowflakes were nestled in the trees. The squirrels would gather around the base of the bird feeder for morsels of food dropped by the brave birds who stayed during the winter, hoping to survive until spring. Thankfully, this year, we all made it through another winter.

Due to my husband's Parkinson's disease, we had closed our business a few years earlier, and now we enjoyed the luxury of sleeping a little later because we no longer had to rise at the break of dawn. Therefore, when I turned to greet my husband good morning, I found it unusual to see him standing in our bathroom doorway instead of resting comfortably in our bed.

Something wasn't right about his appearance and his behavior. He looked somewhat dazed and anxious.

Instinctively, I got up to turn on the light. When I reached for his arm to steady him, he was deep in thought. Because I didn't know what was wrong, I slowly guided him to our bed and asked him to sit down. As I knelt down in front of him, I lifted his chin and saw a worried sadness in his eyes. In order to help him, I asked him to tell me what was wrong.

For a minute, he sat motionless before he described his problem. Since he was not one to complain or tell me things he knew would worry me, I quickly understood he needed to see a doctor when he said, "I am dying. My dad died when he was 69 . . . and so will I."

At first, I was shocked. I was taken aback and said, "You are not dying. Don't worry, everything will be OK."

Now, I was frightened! When I suggested we immediately go to the hospital, he hesitated. Instead of agreeing with me, he insisted, "Maybe we should wait and see if the symptoms clear up on their own."

Usually I would go along with his strategy, but not this time. I knew it was an emergency and persisted in my suggestion that we go to the hospital right away. Although he was still uncertain as to what he should do, he finally agreed with me.

Because he wouldn't let me call an ambulance, I rushed him to the local hospital emergency room myself. As we entered the waiting area, his skin color was pale, and he was unsteady on his feet. Due to his instability, I suggested he sit down while I provided the medical information at the reception desk. After his paperwork was finalized, he was taken into the examination area to evaluate his condition.

I was asked to wait outside the cubicle while the staff began to check my husband's vitals and draw blood for a lab workup. Once it was determined that his condition wasn't critical, at least for the moment, I was allowed to join him to keep him company. During this time, we chatted optimistically about his health issue being a minor inconvenience, anticipating an early discharge so our life would get back to normal. In the meantime, we felt somewhat relieved knowing he was now in experienced hands.

The fact that no emergency medical action was taken helped calm our nerves and lessened his anxiety. Yet, it seemed like an eternity before we learned he had been diagnosed with blood loss from an unknown origin. When the emergency room doctor decided my husband should be admitted in order to determine the cause, an IV was administered.

Since nothing else could be done for him until he was assigned a room and a doctor to review his case, he was rolled out of the emergency room examination area. His gurney was placed in an alcove, located at the dead-end corridor off a small hallway, in front of the now vacant examination room. Because of our obscure location, we were isolated from the normal stressful activities of the ER. We felt as though we were in our own little world, so instead of worrying, we concentrated on our private optimistic conversations which helped eliminate the thought of possible serious health issues.

While we waited for a hospital bed, to make sure he remained stable, the staff regularly monitored his vitals and his blood was routinely drawn.

After a few hours, we were brought back to reality when a hospital aide arrived to inform us a room was now ready. Without a moment's hesitation, my husband was whisked off down the hall with me following dutifully behind.

We took a turn to the left and then to the right before passing through an automatic door which led us out of the emergency room area into the main hospital hallway. Within a few more steps, we were in front of the elevator which brought us to the floor where his room was located.

Before long, we exited the elevator and headed down a hall, through an open door, past the nurses' station and into a semi-private room, which was currently unoccupied. My husband had been assigned a bed by the window, with a pleasant view overlooking an outside parking lot where the oak and maple trees were starting to bloom. He was told to get into bed once he changed from his street clothes into the standard hospital garb he had been given. After he settled in, he was hooked up to the room monitor, and his mobile IV was set into place next to the hospital bed. Finally, he was able to relax.

Not exactly the comforts of home, but this location would be our war room where the battle for his life would begin.

To date, all of his medical services had been provided him through the Providence VA because of the Agent Orange exposure he was subjected to during his service in Vietnam. When I spoke to a VA representative later that morning, I was told that as soon as his emergency condition stabilized and he was released from the hospital, he would be required to return to the VA facility for treatment in the event he needed further medical services.

A hospital physician had already been assigned to his case, and it was determined a biopsy needed to be performed to establish the cause of the bleeding. The operation would take place early that afternoon to render the results. In the meantime, my husband would be monitored on a 24-hour a day basis, according to the nurse on duty, until a diagnosis was determined.

Fortunately, my husband had not eaten since the evening before, so the administration of anesthesia wouldn't be an issue.

When he was taken to the operating room to complete the procedure, I was allowed to wait in his room while the biopsy was performed. I found it impossible to find any interest in the array of shows available on the TV; but the audio sounds, from a nondescript show on the station my husband had been watching, kept me company as I anxiously awaited his return.

Time dragged on while I looked aimlessly out the window, and I tried desperately to think about encouraging thoughts. Unfortunately, my husband's words, "I am dying," spoken softly in the shadows of our bedroom earlier that morning, kept creeping into my mind.

What if he was right? What if there was no simple fix? The what ifs were destroying my anticipation of a positive outcome.

Finally, I heard his cheerful voice in the hallway.

Within a few seconds, I could see his smiling face as his wheelchair was guided through the doorway by a friendly aide. The sound of his voice suggested encouraging news, which raised my hopes for a speedy recovery. The *what ifs* quickly faded from my mind and were replaced by my desire to hear the news that brought the turnaround in his attitude.

My husband spoke optimistically while negotiating his way back into bed, all the while dealing with the nurse's rearrangement of his monitor and IV in order to allow him to get comfortable. From what I could gather, a bleeding ulcer was the culprit. What my husband failed to reveal was that the ulcer might be at risk of rupturing, which could be fatal.

At the time of the procedure, the doctor told my husband he would rush the pathology results, and my husband was under the impression they wouldn't be available until the following day. As far as we both were concerned, the delay wasn't an issue. The results were just a formality. The words *bleeding ulcer* weren't the end of the world, or at least that is what we thought.

Once he got settled in and the nurse left us alone, he appeared to get comfortable as we began to talk enthusiastically about our tomorrows. We looked forward to an imminent discharge and a return of normalcy to our lives.

As the afternoon turned into early evening, my love suggested it was time for me to go home, take care of our dogs, and get something to eat. He knew I didn't want to go, but he preferred that I drove home while there was still some daylight. He didn't like the idea of me arriving home to a dark, empty house.

While leaning over to gently kiss him goodbye, I told him I would be back early the next morning, but I would call to let him know I made it home safely.

During my drive home, while cautiously anticipating that the results of the biopsy would provide good news, I prayed to God, "Please let him be okay."

As I continued to implore God's help in my meditative state, the miles I unconsciously traveled obviously didn't register because suddenly, I was home.

Our house stood prominently at the end of a long, spiraling driveway, set apart from my neighbors and nestled in-between evergreens and oak trees. For the first time, I realized how lonely it felt to come home alone.

After unlocking the door to the house and entering the kitchen, before attending to any other responsibilities, I called my husband to tell him I had made it home safely. While we spoke, it was difficult to sound optimistic because I was so worried during my drive home. Our conversation didn't last long because he was tired from the stressful events of the day, and he wasn't the type of person who enjoyed talking on the phone.

Now satisfied that my husband knew I was safe and sound, I took care of my responsibilities while my thoughts were consumed with fear of the unknown. Evening quickly turned into night, and once I had climbed into bed alone, the quiet solitude and loneliness hurt beyond belief. Darkness was my companion as a troubled sleep overtook my uncertainties, and exhaustion won out over my anguish.

Suddenly it was morning, and time for me to rise, dress, feed the dogs and return to the hospital. Even though I felt certain my husband would be coming home that afternoon, in the back of my mind, I thought it better to be safe than sorry. So I put all the appropriate exterior lights on, before I headed out the door, in the event it became necessary for me to come home alone again for yet another night.

During the drive to the hospital, my thoughts fluctuated between the positives and negatives of our situation. I remember thinking, if he was well, the doctor should have let him come home yesterday. On the other hand, I found comfort in the thought that in this day and age all doctors must proceed on the side of caution. I could only hope I would be welcomed with good news when I arrived.

My husband greeted me with a smile as I walked into his room. Once I reached his side, I leaned over to lovingly kiss him good morning. I was one of the fortune ones, after all these years, there was still magic in his kiss. While I pulled up the chair to sit down next to him, he told me the doctor had already been in to see him. As it turned out, the pathology report couldn't provide a positive diagnosis; however, the doctor indicated precancerous cells were present. When I pressed for further details, my husband said that was all the doctor had told him.

This revelation compelled me to go to the nurses' station, where I left a message for the doctor to contact us, so we could talk about what we should expect next.

Breakfast was being served on his floor when I arrived, so I was surprised to see my husband hadn't been given anything to eat. Up until now, the IV was his only form of nourishment, and it had been over 24-hours since he had eaten. This led me to believe there were still undisclosed concerns lurking beyond our current knowledge regarding the seriousness of his medical condition.

Meanwhile, I did my best to carry on an optimistic conversation about how things were going at home, whereas in the back of my mind, I was extremely concerned.

An uneasy feeling came over me when the doctor entered the room with a serious look on his face. He told us there was a strong possibility the ulcer was cancerous, even though the results weren't conclusive at this time. He recommended a CAT scan be performed to provide additional information upon which he would formulate a more thorough diagnosis.

The news was shocking. What we initially believed to be a minor problem had suddenly become life threatening. The dreaded word cancer was in the mix. Unexpectedly, my hopefulness had now been replaced by fear and anxiety.

Though not in agreement with the suggested diagnosis, to put the matter to rest, my husband decided to have a CAT scan performed. The doctor wasted no time and scheduled the scan immediately. I remember feeling sick to my stomach when he was wheeled out of the room a short time thereafter.

It felt like an eternity before he returned. My nerves settled a little when he came into the room displaying a smirk on his face to cheer me up. He knew how to make me laugh, and it worked. We both benefited from his sense of humor because his ability to make light of a difficult situation was infectious. Unbeknownst to him, his carefree reactions were helping me deal with the catastrophic events taking shape in our lives.

At the time, little did I realize my husband's positive attitude was based upon the fact that he truly believed the doctor was wrong.

It didn't take long for the doctor to review the findings once the CAT scan results were available because he appeared in the doorway within a short period of time after my husband's return. His unexpected visit didn't sit well with me, for I knew the wheels of progress don't turn so quickly when all is well.

The doctor got right to the point, quickly! The results of the procedure confirmed that my husband had an ulcerated gastric body mass which appeared to have invaded the pancreatic wall as well as his stomach. Based upon his educated opinion, the doctor was convinced the mass was cancerous. Now, he wanted to perform a second biopsy because he thought the previous sample taken had not penetrated deep enough into the tumor to confirm his original diagnosis.

Every conference the doctor held with us seemed to bring more concerns to the table. If the doctor was correct, time was of the essence as far as my husband's chances for survival were concerned. So, hoping a conclusive diagnosis could be ascertained, a second emergency biopsy had now been scheduled.

Fully aware the doctor was concerned about the possibility of a rupture of my husband's ulcer, I waited near the operating room in case an emergency occurred during the procedure. It was a small, quiet room, with long glass windows which looked out onto the corridor. I watched as the doctors, nurses, patients and visitors passed by, going on with their busy lives, unaware of the life-changing events going on in mine.

Although there were people all around me, I felt abandoned. All I could do to get through the agonizing waiting period was pray. Over and over, I begged God, "Dear Lord, please have mercy and don't take him away from me!"

Eventually a nurse, in her crisp white uniform, stood in front of me and said, "You can go to see your husband now. He is awake and asking for you."

Words couldn't express how happy I was that he made it through the procedure. Like a lost puppy, I followed the nurse till she led me to the recovery area. When she pulled back the white curtain, our eyes met.

As I slowly walked over to sit by my husband's side, my mind was filled with concern for the outcome of the procedure. I took his hand into mine and held it tightly. He squeezed my hand in return as if to say, everything would be fine. At that moment, our touch said more than words could ever say.

Up until this point, we had managed to uphold our confidence, but now there was little we could say to comfort each other because of the severity of the situation. Our emotions were too raw.

The recovery room was empty, except for the bed in which my husband was recuperating. Since it was already late in the day, the time had come for him to leave the recovery area and be transported back to his room. Though still groggy, he was transferred into a waiting wheelchair for the journey.

As he was rolled down the winding hallways, the noises of the ongoing hospital activities were in stark contrast to the solitude of the diffused environment of the recovery room we had just left.

Life seemed to have brightened as we traveled the short distance to his awaiting hospital bed. My husband quickly displayed his optimistic side once we were no longer alone. He was always so careful not to let others see inside his world. He joked with the aide as she maneuvered him through the hallways and carefully avoided the many people who traveled the same route.

Only a small light was lit above his bed as we entered his room. The evening shades had just begun to overshadow his bed and beckoned him into the coziness of a long-awaited rest.

The anesthesia hadn't fully worn off, and he was extremely tired after all of the tests he had been through during the past two days. He apologized when he told me, "It has been a long day for both of us," which indicated that he wanted me to go home because he could barely keep his eyes open.

He was right. I, too, was physically and mentally exhausted.

So, I kissed him goodbye and left thinking, life is rarely predictable. I could only hope tomorrow would bring some desperately needed good news.

CHAPTER 7

No Dreams to Dream,
No Future to Plan

It was lonely walking the short distance from the hospital's front entrance to my car. When I got in and started the engine, my mind was distant. My emotions were drained. All I wanted was for this awful chapter in our lives to be a terrible mistake.

Once I pulled out of the parking lot, my sadness deepened as I drove home with a heavy heart. I didn't look forward to another lonely night, and the house felt empty as I walked through the door.

Our home had been built with love. There was always a feeling of warmth and goodness which radiated from within its walls. I felt at peace whenever my husband and I were home together.

Now that I was alone, our home was no longer my refuge. Suddenly, it was just a place to sleep, shower, or get a quick bite to eat. How desperately I needed my husband's company to make my life complete.

While evening stretched into night, I worried and prayed for positive results. I could only hope good news would be forthcoming upon my return to the hospital.

Anxious to be back with my husband, I arose early, hurried through my morning activities, and quickly left home for my

20-minute drive to the hospital. Because of my early arrival, I had no difficulty finding a convenient parking space under the shade of one of the small oak trees which lined the outer perimeter of the lot.

As soon as I entered his room, my husband was quick to tell me he had already spoken to the doctor before I arrived. The doctor said the second biopsy results were also inconclusive. My husband enthusiastically added, he would be coming home the next day.

The relief I felt at that moment was beyond description, even though I realized he was not out of hot water by any stretch of the imagination. There was still the issue of his bleeding ulcer.

Shortly after my arrival, a nurse came into the room. She told us the doctor had recommended my husband be given a blood transfusion before he was discharged. Apparently his body had not replenished enough of his own blood to make up for the loss he had sustained. She educated us about the danger he faced because of his lack of a sufficient amount of blood in his system and warned that he was at a high risk of fainting under any form of exertion, which could cause physical harm. Even standing up or walking, without assistance, could be hazardous. She announced that this was the main reason he had been confined to bed during his entire stay.

During our discussion, the nurse provided us with a pamphlet describing the perils one can encounter when a blood transfusion was administered. Despite the fact we believed there was no alternative choice, the nurse left us alone to read the pamphlet and consider the pros and cons of his situation.

We both agreed, if he wanted to go home, the benefits far outweighed the risks. A few minutes later, when the nurse returned, my husband decided to follow the doctor's recommendation. She immediately left the room to prepare for the transfusion and said it would be a short while before the blood would be available.

While we waited, my husband indicated that he had something to tell me. It had to do with an inspirational message one of the nurses thought might be helpful to us in our current situation. Though my husband paraphrased the story, he reported that earlier this morning, the on-duty nurse wanted us to realize we were given a gift.

I listened intently, as he continued with the narrative. She encouraged him by her depiction of the many observations she experienced in her life as a nurse. She explained how many people die instantaneously from a car accident, an unexpected heart attack, or some other serious malady; and yet, she asserted, we still had some precious time left to be together and prepare, no matter what the outcome.

My husband wanted to pass on her story, so I could find comfort in her message as well. His caring words to me were, "In the event my time turns out to be limited, at least we still have some time to prepare ourselves for the worst-case scenario, while hoping for the best."

During this difficult interval, my husband thought we should cherish each moment we still had together. He wanted us to continue enjoying the good our lives had to offer, instead of dwelling upon the bad. I will never forget the compassionate effort he made to comfort me that day.

Throughout our ordeal, we often recalled the significance of the message this caring nurse had shared with my husband, in her attempt to console her patient, whom she knew was gravely ill. Unbeknownst to her, throughout the many days we had trouble coping with our situation, she had provided lasting encouragement for us both.

Our conversation was interrupted when the nurse returned to administer the blood transfusion. After the procedure was completed, she stated that my husband should see improvement in his stability within a short period of time. Then, she left to take care of her other responsibilities, a never-ending list of assignments every nurse needs to accomplish throughout the day.

Since we were both looking forward to his release the next morning, we now felt one step closer to that goal. Finally, we believed things were progressing in a positive direction.

We found ourselves alone again, and we began to discuss what plans needed to be implemented from this point forward. By virtue of our own consensus, we believed the inconclusive results of both biopsies indicated there was a good chance the ulcer hadn't become cancerous as of yet, and his VA doctors would figure out a cure.

For the time being, hopefully a little bit of sunshine had finally come our way. Then, the doctor's assistant walked in and spoiled our expectations.

At first, we assumed she had stopped by to provide an overview of my husband's discharge information, but that didn't turn out to be the case. Instead, she recapped the doctor's warning of the high probability that my husband had pancreatic cancer, and she insisted he needed immediate medical attention while the window of opportunity still existed. She reiterated the urgency of his condition and strongly recommended he make an appointment with an oncologist for Monday to begin chemotherapy treatment.

Even though her insistence alarmed me, her perseverance made no sense. Although I was concerned, her appeals were irrelevant because we already had an appointment scheduled for Monday with my husband's primary care doctor at the VA in Providence. In order for his medical bills to be paid, it was essential for my husband to be treated through the VA system. His emergency care, at this hospital, was an exception to the VA's rule due to extenuating circumstances.

My husband was getting upset as she continued her onslaught of, what we believed to be, an exaggeration of his condition. No matter how many times he reminded her that the biopsy results were inconclusive, she kept insisting he take her advice. Having reached his boiling point he heatedly told her, whatever treatment needed to be done would be remedied through the VA medical system. He was upset because she wouldn't take no for an answer.

It was obvious that she was frustrated as well. She finally left because she didn't want to stress out my husband any further.

Though confused by her objective, I didn't want to think about the implications of her conversation. In order to get through the weekend, we needed to hold onto whatever hope we had been able to muster up until that moment. Therefore, we ignored her opinions and managed to get into an upbeat, heart-to-heart exchange about how wonderful tomorrow would be, when we were home together again. Just like in a fairytale story, we somehow managed to successfully tuck away our doubts and create a make-believe world where everything would turn out fine. It was all we could do to tolerate the unthinkable.

Our plan to stabilize his ulcer, in preparation for the long drive to the VA in Providence, was our primary concern. While deciding upon his homecoming strategy, I told my husband I would stop at the grocery store to stock up on provisions on my way home that afternoon. Once I put the food away and fed the dogs, I would return to the hospital and keep him company for his last night's stay.

After giving him a quick kiss goodbye, I headed down the hospital hallway. When I reached the elevator, my cell phone rang. It was the doctor's assistant on the other end, and the tone in her voice was alarming. She wanted to speak to me about the doctor's assessment of my husband's health situation, because she was concerned he had rejected the strong probability that he had cancer. Since she thought that I was more open to the gravity of his situation, she wanted to talk to me without upsetting him.

My heart pounded inside my chest as she spoke. After I pressed her further, she finally admitted that the doctor suspected my husband had aggressive pancreatic cancer. When I asked her, "How much time did he have left if this information was correct?"

She replied, "Six months to a year."

Because she felt obligated to make sure we did something about his health issue, she persisted in her warning that we not ignore the gravity of the situation he was in. She ended our conversation by emphasizing . . . if my husband did nothing, he would die sooner rather than later.

I choked up and could no longer speak as tears welled up in my eyes. To hide my distress, I stared out the window next to me and hoped no one noticed my despair. Overcome with grief, I composed myself as best I could. Nothing had prepared me for this anguish. At that moment, my life fell to pieces!

Now, I had to return to my husband's side and share this overwhelming revelation. While I rushed back down the corridors, I tried to calm down, but my husband knew my footsteps and could tell the sound of urgency in my walk. When I appeared in the doorway, he knew something must be terribly wrong for me to have returned so unexpectedly.

Instantly, I rushed into his arms. He held me tight while I tried to convey the life-shattering news through my sobs.

He was the strong one. He comforted me, even though he was the one facing death. Despite the fact that he was the one with the fatal illness, I felt like I was dying too.

As he held me close, he told me he wasn't upset and would accept whatever was meant to be. While a storm of destruction formed around us, my love was the one to calm the seas. He actually seemed to be at peace with the journey which lay ahead and affectionately reassured me: although our future was uncertain, he was not dead yet.

At the moment, all I could do was nod my head in agreement because I didn't want to leave the security of his embrace.

In the midst of our anguish, we agreed to do everything we could to beat his illness.

Finally, I calmed down to the point where I just felt numb. In response to my despondency, once again my husband reminded me that the biopsy results were inconclusive.

Gradually, I drew upon his strength and agreed wholeheartedly with his optimistic point of view. Now, I gravitated toward a positive outcome because I was terrified of the negative one. We decided we would not accept defeat before learning all of the facts, and we agreed that we had to tackle the beast head on.

On the upside, my love was coming home, and we would deal with our tomorrows as they came.

Overwhelmed by the disclosure, it took awhile before my husband could convince me to leave. I was torn between my responsibility to get everything ready for his return home and my fear of losing him. I needed time to grasp the severity of our situation. The thought of the possibility of life without him was inconceivable. God forgive me, I wished it were me instead of him!

Despite the fact that my husband tried desperately to hide his true feelings from me, the devastating news we learned that day had an undesirable effect on him. Even though we had not given up hope, his demeanor changed in subtle ways. It was now evident that all the wants and desires he always sought, around which our lives had evolved, were no longer in his future. Slowly, his optimistic approach to life vanished, like the childhood belief in Santa Clause which eventually comes to an end.

As time passed, I sensed the anguish in his conviction that he had no more dreams to dream, no future to plan.

CHAPTER 8

The Revelation

During my husband's hospital stay, we decided against inviting visitors because we needed time to digest the relentless influx of information which constantly bombarded us. Currently, we had no idea what to expect, so we didn't want to deal with questions for which we had no answers. My husband and I agreed, visitors would make the circumstances worse by adding extra stress to an already difficult situation.

Additionally, we didn't want the increased burden of deliberating between family opinions and doctor recommendations since we already had more than enough information to process. It would have been too exhausting to deal with.

In between the chaotic chain of events which had taken over our lives during his diagnostic period at the hospital, we welcomed the solitary peace and quiet we were able to share.

While he rested in his hospital bed, with his toes peeking out from under the white sheets because the room was too warm, I sat in the straight back chair near the window, periodically looking out. I longingly dreamed of the day he would be coming home. During these times when his room was quiet, except for the beeps of his heart monitor, we managed to talk about an optimistic future which enabled us to cope with the doctor's proposed diagnosis.

While we were used to facing adversity in our lives, and we never backed away from a challenge, this time it was different.

Even though our discussions were positive and we believed everything was going to be fine, we understood my husband's current limitations and realized we couldn't handle matters on our own without the assistance of outside help.

Since I had just obtained the doctor's perilous interpretation of my husband's proposed diagnosis from his assistant, it dramatically changed our approach to addressing his illness. Although my husband's fragile ulcer condition was definitely a serious issue to contend with, as far as we were concerned, the cancer prognosis wasn't conclusive. During my husband's entire hospital confinement, he had not been allowed out of bed without assistance. This meant, once he got home, he would be in no condition to do anything except rest, and I needed to make sure he did just that.

Since my husband had experienced a dramatic health scare, it understandably enabled me to convince him to stay home to recuperate, in order to give his ulcer time to heal. Therefore, to accomplish this goal, we both agreed it would be best to call my sister and her husband to ask if they would help us.

Rationally thinking, were we to have told anyone about my husband's condition, it would have been them. But at the time, on the same day my husband had been hospitalized, my brother-in-law was having tests performed at another hospital to resolve a health concern of his own. Since my brother-in-law's tests had required him to stay overnight, and we weren't sure how he made out, we hadn't reached out to them as of yet. On my way home from the hospital today, I planned to call my sister to make sure her husband was OK before I unloaded our problems upon them.

With a plan in mind, I told my husband I would be back later that afternoon after I spoke with my sister, picked up the mail and took care of the essential matters at home.

I struggled emotionally every time I had to leave him. The only consoling thought I was able to seize upon was that I would be returning to his side after I took care of my obligations. Every action I executed felt like an automatic response, similar to the Pavlov dog theory, from years of operative conditioning. I was amazed how robotic a person could become when their brain was overwhelmed under such circumstances.

As I prepared to leave, I smiled as I grabbed my keys, leaned over to steal a kiss, and said, "I'll see you soon," before I turned and walked out of his room.

Riding the elevator had become a mindless activity, and it didn't take long until I reached the outside of the building. The sun was bright and much warmer than earlier that morning when my foggy ride to the hospital seemed to match my bewildered state of mind.

By the time I reached my car, I had to take off my jacket. I threw it into the unoccupied front seat since the interior had warmed up considerably from the heat of the sun, compared to the nip in the air earlier in the day. When I turned the engine on, I lowered the thermostat to allow air conditioning to replace the heat I had craved on my way to the hospital.

All these actions were just a distraction from what was really on my mind. It was time to face the music and call my sister. Our discussion would have to take place while I was on the road, so I would have this difficult conversation behind me. Before I pulled out of the parking lot, I hit the automatic key on my cell phone to dial her home number, which I had already connected through my car's hands-free system. When the phone began to ring, my car was already in gear, and I was headed home.

My sister answered the phone on the second ring. After our greeting pleasantries were over, I asked how her husband made out. She happily replied, "Everything was fine!"

It was at this point, I took a deep breath and struggled to tell her about my husband's health problems. At first, I explained how we ended up at the hospital, early in the morning, two days ago. Next, I filled her in regarding his blood loss, biopsies and CAT scan. When it came time to disclose the suspected diagnosis of terminal pancreatic cancer . . . I lost it! All I could manage to say, while choking back my tears, was that we needed their help.

45

My account took her by complete surprise since the last time she saw us my husband looked fine. While trying to digest my heart-wrenching report, her voice became silent. Once she understood the revelation, she herself broke down.

Finally, in an audibly upset response, she asked, "What can we do?"

Before I could answer her question, she immediately inquired if they should come to the hospital, but I replied, "No, he didn't want any company."

My husband and I preferred to be alone since this would be his last night's stay. We needed peace and quiet, knowing once we started sharing the specifics of his illness with others, we would never be able to put the cork back into the bottle.

I told her that we would discuss our needs once I ironed them out with my husband. However, before we ended our call, I managed to explain that basically, we just needed them to run errands so we could come straight home from the hospital on the day he was discharged. I wanted her to understand the situation and be ready for our call, because as of that moment, we had no particular plan of attack in mind.

By the time I divulged our situation, I was inconsolable and could no longer speak. Now, choking on my words in despair, I meekly told my sister I would call her back the next morning when we were ready to leave the hospital. I didn't want to discuss our situation any longer because I was terrified at the concept of losing the love of my life.

I don't recall much else about the ride home that afternoon, or what I did when I got there. There were surely mundane matters I attended to, but they were insignificant. All I could think about was getting my husband home and cured.

CHAPTER 9

She Was Mad at God

By the time I got back to the hospital, it was already mid-afternoon. The visitor's parking area was packed, a far cry from the availability of spots when I arrived early in the morning. Eventually, I found a space near the outer edge of the lot. Unlike most people, who always try to park close to the entrance, I didn't mind walking, especially on such a beautiful day.

Meanwhile, since it was already Friday, I was thrilled my husband would be coming home the next day. Being optimistic, I assumed the doctor wouldn't let him come home if he wasn't up to it. At least, I hoped so.

By the time I reached my husband's room, he already knew it was me because of the distinctive clicking sound my heels made on the flooring as I walked. Therefore, when I entered the room, he was already smiling in anticipation of my arrival.

Even though he looked tired from all he had been through, it felt good to see him in such an upbeat mood. I guess the thought of going home would make anyone happy.

When I asked what he had eaten for lunch, he replied, "Nothing."

This didn't sit well with me since I thought, if everything was progressing in a positive direction, some food or beverage should have been given to him by now.

He wasn't concerned and just assumed he would get something to eat for supper later that day. He said he wasn't hungry anyway.

What worried me was that maybe the doctor was keeping him on a no-food order in the event some sort of emergency occurred, but, since there was no indication this was the case, I wasn't going to burden my husband with my apprehensive analysis of the situation.

Trying to put this worrisome thought out of my mind, I brought up the conversation I had earlier with my sister. I let him know how upset she was about the news and told him they wanted to come and visit.

He was pleased to hear I explained he was too tired for visitors, and therefore, had advised them not to come. There would be plenty of time to visit when they came to our house tomorrow.

Besides, there was something else on his mind that he wanted to discuss. He thought we needed to tell our daughter and son-in-law about his diagnosis. Since we had already told my sister and her husband, he suggested they should be informed as well.

Of course, I agreed, but I also knew this meant I would be the one elected to make the call. It was hard enough for me to tell my sister the daunting news, but to have to tell our only child that her father's life was in jeopardy would be even more difficult.

By now, it had been a grueling three-day experience, and he was exhausted. After visiting for a short period of time, he imploringly suggested that I go home. He wanted to get some sleep, to strengthen himself for his morning discharge.

He was dozing off while we spoke, so I reluctantly agreed. This time, after I kissed him goodbye, I tiptoed out of the room. I didn't want to disturb him as he fell asleep.

It wasn't easy for me to leave. Although I knew he was due to come home in the morning, his diagnosis made me realize how uncertain our life's survival really is. For the first time, I no longer felt the security in the perpetuation of our lives together, which had always been a certainty in my mind. I no longer felt optimistic for the happiness our tomorrows might bring. One day all was well . . . and then, suddenly, it was not.

My thoughts were troubled as I drove home. Although the highway was bustling with heavy traffic due to the Friday evening commute, I felt as though I was the only person on the road. I dreaded the prospect of the phone call I had to make to our daughter because there was no perfect way to deliver the sad news I needed to convey.

Although years had passed, it didn't seem so long ago since she and her husband had learned about her father's Parkinson's disease. Of course, they already understood her dad would never be the same as she observed his quality of life diminish. But now, God's plans had changed again, and he faced a deadly cancer as well.

By the time I got home, my stomach felt like it was tied in a knot because of the stressful conversation ahead of me. Once I dialed the number, I struggled to keep my composure. Unexpectedly, it was my son-in-law who answered the phone, instead of my daughter. When I asked to speak with her, he told me that she wasn't home from work yet.

There was a nervous tension in his response, followed by silence, as he waited to hear what I had to say. From the tone of my voice, he knew something was terribly wrong. I could barely speak as I choked upon my words.

Since I didn't have the fortitude to make the call twice in order to talk to my daughter directly, I decided to provide my son-in-law with the details regarding her father's illness. This way, once she came home, he could tell her the distressing news.

The conversation was difficult and didn't transpire as smoothly as I had hoped. I tried to be positive and suggested the proposed cancer might only be precancerous at this point. I rattled off a number of potential probabilities which could possibly create an optimistic outcome.

In actuality, I believe I tried to convince myself more than him that everything would turn out fine.

He was stunned. I could hear his anguish when he replied, "I am so sorry."

The strain in his voice was evident when he assured me he would tell her as soon as she arrived. Our call hastily concluded because there was nothing more either one of us was able to say.

Shortly thereafter, my daughter called me back. She already knew the bad news, so we cried and supported each other that night. The normal clichés, things would work out and everything would be fine, were shared between us. Most importantly, we would agree to be optimistic and remain strong, if not for ourselves, for her father. Even though the sky was falling, we were in it together.

My daughter was mad at God. She told me so. She said she couldn't accept the possibility of losing her father. It wasn't fair!

I tried to soothe her anxiety by assuring her that her father had already accepted God's will, whatever it might be. I encouragingly offered my opinion. We all have our own journey to travel in life. When our journey ends, our time on Earth also ends. According to the directive of our voyage on this planet, we are all born to die.

In my attempt to help our daughter deal with her sadness, I offered her the additional explanation: Our God is a God of Love who does not want us to suffer, but we cannot enjoy the tenderness of love without ultimately facing the grief the death of a loved one brings.

Obviously, because death is part of life, my daughter understood that none of us were exempt from this terrible experience.

By the time we finished talking, the house had become dark and lonely. It was time to retire to my room and prepare for bed, in order to get some rest.

As I settled in for the night, my mind was obsessed with thoughts about the future. All I could think about was where our lives were headed, and how much time did we actually have left to be together?

Daybreak came slowly. I had struggled through the night, in fear he would have a medical emergency once he was home, as a result of his bleeding ulcer. However, my desire for us to be together again far outweighed my fears.

Since I knew pancreatic cancer carried a swift death sentence, for now, I refused to accept this prognosis until we were certain there was no other alternative explanation. I reminded myself that I needed to keep a positive outlook and a stiff upper lip for both our sakes. We needed to fight this demon together, for it was impossible to go it alone.

I knew I couldn't let my anxiety override my conviction. I had to believe he would survive and our lives would return to normal.

That morning, when I got up, dressed and headed to the hospital, everything went like clockwork until I reached his room and found my husband still in his hospital garb, hooked up to the heart monitor and IV. Since I knew how anxious he was to be discharged, I realized something was wrong. It was an understatement to say he did not look pleased. I soon learned there was a glitch in the hospital's sign-out paperwork. A doctor my husband hadn't met, whose services were never requested, had failed to sign the sign-off sheet. Obviously, since my husband wasn't this doctor's patient, there was no reason his signature should be required.

It took a little bit of finagling but, after I spoke to the head nurse on duty, she came up with a viable solution and the matter was resolved. The monitor and IV were removed, and my husband was finally allowed to change into his street clothes.

It didn't take long thereafter for the discharge paperwork to be finalized. In the meantime, he relaxed in bed and no longer minded the wait. He knew we would be heading home shortly.

CHAPTER 10

No Stone Unturned

During the time we were waiting for the final details of my husband's discharge to be worked out, I called my sister to let her know we would be on our way soon. I asked if they would meet us at our house within the hour.

I was pleased to see how content my husband looked as he relaxed on the hospital bed, dressed in his pullover knit shirt and blue jeans. His bed was fixed in a sitting position. As he leaned back against the pillows, his legs stretched straight out across the mattress, while his black leather work boots extended off the side so that he wouldn't get any of the polish on the bedsheets.

While we talked, my husband mentioned that he had eaten a small amount of food for breakfast earlier, but not a lot. As part of his discharge plan, a dietician entered the room and informed us that she was supposed to provide a diet for my husband to follow, which was intended to help heal his ulcer.

She had a clipboard and some paperwork with suggested food items to assist us in making proper nutritional choices. With a grin on her face, she said, "I assume you know the difference between healthy food and junk food."

That being said, she went on to discuss food groups we should include in his diet, which would be most beneficial for my husband's fragile bleeding ulcer.

Today was the first of many times my husband would be advised to eat multiple small meals throughout the day, instead of three regular meals. In this particular instance, the advice was intended to keep his stomach from stretching. The dietician explained that the last thing my husband needed was to stretch his stomach and cause the ulcer to bleed again, because it could be life threatening. Once she cautioned us about the severity of his situation, she presented a positive outlook and implied that the food and prescription pills would be beneficial to put my husband's ulcer on the mend.

After she completed all of her instructions, she asked, "Do you have any questions?" In view of the fact she had covered all the bases, we were satisfied we could competently handle his care at home.

Finally, the discharge nurse arrived and provided prescriptions from the doctor for two types of antacid pills, which were only available through a pharmacy. Both were to be taken as prescribed, multiple times throughout the day. Should there be any delay in getting his prescriptions filled, my husband was given a few pills to take home with us. By the time the dietician and nurse explained the multitude of instructions, the final discharge papers were complete.

Shortly thereafter, an aide with a wheelchair arrived to transport my husband to the freedom he had been yearning for. Ready to go home, he cautiously settled into the chair. Once he was comfortable, I looked around the room to make sure we hadn't forgotten anything. I handed him a plastic bag which contained a few personal essentials, along with the prescriptions and nutritional information we had been given. When I asked if he was ready to leave, he promptly said, "Let's go."

Words couldn't describe how happy he looked when the aide wheeled him out of his hospital room for the last time, and we headed toward the elevator. I saw a combination of relief, anticipation and contentment in his eyes, all wrapped into one. His smile said it all, "I'm going home."

Once we made our way to the outside patio, at the hospital's front entrance, he waited with the aide while I walked over to retrieve our car. After unlocking the driver's door, I sat down, put on my seatbelt, started the engine, took a deep breath, and thanked God he was alive.

The clouds had covered the sun, so there was a bit of a chill in the air, but as I drove up to where he was waiting the sun came out. After shutting off the engine, I got out of the car and walked over to open the front passenger door, when a pleasant feeling came over me. The thought that I wouldn't have to spend another night alone without him warmed my heart.

I could tell he was weak because he got up slowly out of the wheelchair. Once standing, my husband managed to grab the car's hand support bar to pull himself into the vehicle, while his aide stood behind him to prevent him from falling. After he got into the car, I waited to make sure he fastened his seat belt. Now satisfied all was well, I got into the driver's seat, buckled up, put the car into gear, and we were on our way.

As I pulled out of the parking lot, I took a left at the first light, then a left at the second light, and soon we were on the highway. It was smooth sailing from there. Within 15 or 20 minutes, we would be home.

It felt odd for me to be driving with my husband as the passenger, instead of the other way around, but he was in no shape to drive, and we both knew it.

Once we were on the open road, we talked about how much easier it would be for him to recuperate in the comfort of our own home, without him having to worry about me being home alone. He apologized for his illness and the medical difficulties which lay ahead, and he said he would be lost if anything ever happened to me.

His words saddened me, so I told him that life had a way of presenting difficult obstacles from time to time. This just happened to be our time.

Because we had been so deeply engrossed in our conversation, it seemed like no time at all before we reached the end of the cul-de-sac where we lived. As I drove down the driveway, I glanced over at him. His expression of tranquility reassured me. It appeared his stress level had dropped immensely since he looked so relaxed. It amazed me how coming home had such a calming effect upon him.

I asked him to remain seated as I pulled into the garage because I wanted to be near him before he got out of the car . . . just in case. He threw me one of his, you've got to be kidding looks, but obliged.

Since this would be his first attempt to walk on his own, without a walker or wheelchair to support him, I wanted to be sure he was steady on his feet. Once I was standing next to him, he slipped out of his seat, and I looped my arm through his before we walked into the house together. After we reached the kitchen center island, he turned to me and said, "It feels so good to be home!" Putting my arms around him, I hugged him and lovingly replied, "That is an understatement."

It felt strange, yet wonderful at the same time, to have him home again. His absence for the past three days, and my travels between our house and the hospital, made his physical presence at home feel more like a wonderful dream, than reality.

I asked if he wanted something to eat, but he said he was more tired than hungry and just wanted to relax. He then walked into the family room, where he immediately settled into a comfortable chair and turned on the TV.

A few minutes later, I peeked around the corner to check on him, and he was fast asleep. It was the most peaceful I had seen him in days.

Within the hour, my sister and her husband arrived. As they entered the house, they hugged me for moral support. I had no positive updated information to soothe the look of concern on their faces because my husband's preliminary diagnosis wasn't good, and they knew it.

Upon entering the house, they asked where my husband was. I told them he was resting in the family room. While the three of us walked into the kitchen together, as though nothing was wrong, my husband came around the corner to say hello.

Despite the fact he looked healthy on the outside, I was uncertain if lurking on the inside, a catastrophe was unfolding.

To make the situation less stressful, my husband invited everyone to come and sit outside, under the covered front porch. Somehow, the sunshine always seemed to make things seem better than they actually were.

After my husband sat down in one of the two lawn chairs we always kept out front, I grabbed two folding chairs from the inside hall closet and set them outside. Now, everyone had a seat to relax in.

The conversation started out on a positive note because, like the sunshine, my husband's optimistic attitude was refreshing, especially since he was convinced he didn't have cancer. It enabled all of us to carry on with an optimistic frame of mind.

Soon, the dialog evolved into a discussion about my husband's bleeding ulcer. It still boggles my mind when I think of how his ulcer had been diagnosed as pancreatic cancer. I always thought ulcers were just a nuisance which, from time to time, needed treatment.

When it came to the thought of dealing with such a deadly disease, it was frightening. Still, my husband was right about one thing. So far, his biopsies were inconclusive, and we needed to remain hopeful.

My sister and her husband asked what they could do to help, and the answer was simple. Since my husband's diagnosis required rest, a proper diet and medication, we needed them to run our errands until his ulcer stabilized.

We also wanted to find out if the prognosis he received from the hospital physician was verifiable. Starting Monday, the VA doctors would play an important role in determining an accurate diagnosis. In the meantime, I wanted our own research information to better prepare for his upcoming appointments.

This was where my sister and her husband's help was indispensable. They scoured the internet and assembled valuable medical information which helped us understand what we were up against. In time, I took over this monumental task, but for the moment, even though I tried not to show it, I was too traumatized to be of much help.

When we began to discuss my husband's nutritional needs, because we had never been health food enthusiasts, we sought my sister and brother-in-law's advice. While my husband and I ate nutritional cuisine at local restaurants, as well as our own home-cooked meals, our diet was neither organic nor non-GMO foods. Although junk food was not high on our list, we did eat it occasionally.

Fortunately for us, their expertise in this matter began a number of years ago. At my brother's recommendation, my sister and her husband converted to eating organic foods because it was healthier. Since we weren't the type of family to impose our life's choices upon others, no one forced their eating habits upon us. Now that we were asking for advice, this was the first place my sister and brother-in-law suggested we start.

The three most highly recommended changes they advocated were: eat organic food, juice organic vegetables and add specific homeopathic remedies, as recommended. The juicing enabled my husband to gain nutritional benefits from certain vegetables, which offered healing qualities for his ulcer without having to eat large amounts of each food category. For decades, my sister and brother-in-law had utilized juicing for their own health issues, with positive results.

The dietician highly recommended eating small amounts of food per meal, per day. Once my sister and her husband began to deliver organic chicken, vegetables and fresh clams, I prepared homemade organic chicken soup and clam chowder. When my husband didn't have the appetite to eat solid foods, the broth provided nutritional benefits which delivered the nourishment required to help keep him alive.

It might have been late in the game to make a substantial difference in the outcome, but we felt the change in his eating habits would be advantageous overall. Our goal was to heal his ulcer, provide the highest quality nutrients possible and strengthen his immune system.

We were already familiar with the benefits of homeopathy. Many day-to-day remedies and healing ointments were being implemented to prevent colds, soothe poison ivy, bug bites, muscle pain, and nerve damage. Certain natural cures were used to help promote healing by accelerating the normal repair process performed by the body.

Originally, my husband was not a fan of natural remedies, but long ago he succumbed to my sister's way of thinking which he affectionately nicknamed *voodoo medicine.* While the name stuck, the treatment eventually became acceptable.

Despite believing in the benefits of homeopathy, we understood that a serious disease like cancer couldn't be treated through this method alone.

Our immune system is complicated and therefore, we agreed to do everything possible to aid in his recovery and try to promote better health. We would continue our efforts to combat my husband's illness even if we had no guarantee of a successful outcome. We would leave no stone unturned in our effort to extend his life.

I can never thank my sister and brother-in-law enough for all the time and energy they lovingly and generously provided in their never-ending efforts to help us!

CHAPTER 11

Suggestive Suppositions

My sister and brother-in-law went shopping on Saturday afternoon to purchase homeopathic supplies, vitamins and organic foods in our attempt to build up my husband's immune system and strength. When they came back on Sunday, to drop off the provisions they had so carefully collected, my sister and her husband kept their visit short, so that my husband wouldn't get exhausted.

Their gracious assistance, at a time when my husband and I both needed to calm down, to relax and spend precious time together, allowed my husband the liberty to not feel guilty, because he now knew that all of these responsibilities were no longer mine alone to bear.

After all, if I had to run all of our errands, while insisting that my husband stay at home, alone, and relax, he never would have done that. We were both fully aware that the time we spent together could no longer be counted on as a continuing fact of life, and neither one of us wanted to lose any of the valuable time we had left to be together.

Before my husband was discharged on Saturday, I had stopped by the hospital's medical records office to pick up the reports and test results for his three day stay. I wanted to read the attending physician's notes, in order to get a clearer picture of my husband's diagnosis before our Monday morning appointment with his primary care doctor at the VA.

Our weekend together was quiet and peaceful because my husband slept most of the time. The nurse at the hospital, who had administered the blood transfusion, said he would continue to be tired since the one unit of blood he received wouldn't be quite enough to bring his blood levels back to the amount required for normal bodily functions. Once the bleeding stopped, the passage of time would allow his body to replace the blood he had lost. In the interim, rest and relaxation was his best medicine.

It was calming for me to sit on the loveseat in our family room and look over to see my husband comfortably stretched out on the couch. I now treasured the simple pleasure of watching him sleep because I no longer assumed his life was as indestructible as I had always believed.

While he slept or watched TV, I kept my laptop up and running. I researched pancreatic cancer, as well as other unfamiliar words in his test results, to try and figure out what these words meant. I wanted to understand what hidden messages were in these reports, why the doctor was so convinced my husband had this deadly disease, and most importantly . . . I questioned why now, when we were just getting our lives back in order after his Parkinson's diagnosis?

Upon reviewing the reports, they were inconclusive and merely theorized that his diagnosis suspected pancreatic cancer. They were full of suggestive suppositions because all they proposed were guesses, theories or possibilities.

For me, that wasn't enough. I wanted proof before I would believe that God would take him away from me, especially knowing I couldn't live without him!

It was just that the proof I sought was the exact opposite of what the doctor theorized. I needed to know my husband would be okay.

Millions of thoughts ran through my mind during the long agonizing wait for Monday to arrive, but none of them could convenience me that he was, or should I say, we were facing one of the deadliest cancers known to mankind.

So, I held onto hope for a positive outcome because there were holes in the reports that didn't seem to hold water. Two biopsies, in two days, didn't seem to be convincing evidence in my opinion, since neither biopsy confirmed the death sentence his doctor had suggested. Therefore, my husband had to be right . . . he would be fine.

Even if on the outside chance the ulcer was pre-cancerous, God would heal him . . . or so I prayed.

I needed to keep busy because you know what they say, "An idle mind is the devil's workshop." To hold onto my sanity, I worked diligently towards healing his ulcer by preparing high-nutrient, low-density foods for him to eat. I also kept up with his scheduled medication and vitamin supplements to make sure he took everything as prescribed. It was confusing at first, until I drew up a chart which helped me keep track of his pill and food intake.

What made life simpler for me at the time was the fact that my husband agreed to take it easy, at least for the first weekend, because relaxing at home was foreign to him.

He loved the outdoors, so when we weren't driving throughout the countryside, I usually found him outside working. There was always grass to be cut, bushes to trim, all of the typical maintenance homeowners never seem to accomplish . . . and of course, his cars to wash. When it came to his favorite vehicle, a convertible, he always washed and dried it, either before or after each outing.

Then, at the end of what used to be our normal daily routine, we enjoyed what we called a walkabout. That was the time of day, near dusk, when we let the dogs out to run and play alongside my husband and me. We always walked the large open pasture that bordered the oak and hazelnut trees, which covered most of our property. Once the leaves came in, we didn't venture into the woods too often because a bear occasionally roamed throughout our neighborhood. Nevertheless, we always enjoyed seeing the white tails of the deer, pointing up towards the sky, as they scattered from their feasting on the freshly mowed grass in the field out back once they sensed our presence.

Only now, none of these activities were possible. Until my husband was better, even our leisurely late-in-the-day strolls would have to be put on the back burner.

When Monday morning arrived, I didn't feel enough time had passed to put a dent in his healing process, but we had no choice, because our journey to the doctor was a matter of life and death. We took our chances and prayed the strenuous activities of the day wouldn't create any harmful effects upon his health.

My husband's primary care doctor was already aware of his situation because of the information I provided when I requested the emergency appointment. Therefore, when his doctor came out into the waiting room to call us in, we were greeted with a look of concern on his face instead of his usual smile.

The doctor tried to be positive, but after he reviewed the reports I gave him, his unhappy look of concern dampened our spirits. He told us to wait in his office while he went to the oncology department to see what they recommended.

About twenty minutes later, his doctor returned and said it had been determined that my husband needed to see a specialist for an upper endoscopic ultrasound and biopsy. The oncologist needed to confirm if the preliminary diagnosis was correct, so the procedure would be scheduled as soon as possible.

In an attempt to comfort us, his doctor proposed that a course of treatment would be formulated in the event the ulcer was cancerous. Although his primary care doctor provided hope that a solution would be found, my husband was disappointed to learn his case would now be transferred out of this doctor's hands, because he felt his primary care doctor was more than a VA doctor . . . he was a friend.

I remember, before leaving his office, the doctor shook my husband's hand. With a look of deep concern on his face, he wished the both of us luck. There was nothing further he could do.

We left without any feeling of optimism to brighten our drive home. Our misgivings swelled, like the dark menacing clouds that intensify before the destructive forces of a tornado strike. I silently worried about our future as we walked, side by side, to our car.

CHAPTER 12

God Help Us,
We May Need a Miracle!

On Tuesday, a staff member from the VA called to say a biopsy and endoscopic procedure had been scheduled for that Friday. The VA consultant divulged that the doctor was one of the best in his field and just happened to be an attending physician at the Roger Williams Medical Center, located directly across the street from the Providence VA Medical Center.

We had nothing but praise and gratitude for the special effort put forth by all of the hard-working medical staff of the VA to manipulate schedules in order to squeeze my husband's appointments into the doctors' schedules so promptly.

Encouraged that the wheels of progress were turning so quickly, we wondered if the express track, which brought us to this particular specialist, was some sort of fate or good fortune. Only time would tell.

When Friday finally arrived, our drive to Providence proved unnerving. The fact that my husband's life may depend upon the results these medical procedures revealed was a very difficult thought to process. God help us, depending upon the outcome, we may need a miracle!

Even though we tried to be optimistic and keep our conversation positive, it wasn't a happy trip. As the expression goes, the tension was so thick you could cut it with a knife. Neither one of us wanted to say, or even think, the word cancer, as we drove for over an hour to reach our destination.

As soon as we parked the car and walked toward the hospital, it was hard to keep up the pretense that everything was fine.

A small waiting room was located on the first floor, just a short distance from the side door we had just entered. There were only three patients ahead of us, so once my husband checked in, it didn't take long before his name was called. We were then led through a locked door into the area where his medical information would be confirmed.

The medical team, who assisted my husband, was extremely pleasant and helpful. They tried their best to put my husband at ease and explained how his outpatient procedure would be performed. We were warned the procedure could be risky because of the fragile condition of his ulcer. They also advised that the side effects of the anesthesia could sometimes be problematic. Both of us were well aware of the dangers.

Once all the pre-op details were completed, we were led back to the waiting room until it was time to perform his third biopsy in ten days.

A little over an hour had passed when it was finally time for him to receive a sedative in preparation for the anesthesia. I knew a prognosis needed to be ascertained, but now that the moment had arrived for my husband to undergo the procedure, I didn't want him taken away, because my concern for his safety had elevated to a crisis mode. I was extremely worried about the perilous risks involved, but there was only enough time for me to give him a quick kiss before he was taken in one direction and I was led in another.

While he was being rolled toward the operating room, I looked back at him longingly, as I was led to the waiting room to begin my vigil. It felt like time stood still, for each time I looked up, the hands on the clock didn't seem to move at all.

As I sat in silence, tears began to trickle down my cheeks. I was terrified of the danger he was in due to his unstable condition. Again, I prayed to God to please not take him from me at this time.

During my wait, an emergency occurred in the procedure area we were in. I heard a call over the speaker system for medical assistance to proceed to our location.

My thoughts immediately turned to the worst-case scenario. Was my husband in eminent danger, was he bleeding uncontrollably, was he at risk?

I didn't go up to the window to inquire about his progress because I felt foolish for being so worried, and I didn't want anyone to see me crying. With my heart racing and tension building inside of me, the thought I could be losing him at that particular moment never felt so real.

However, since time passed, and no one came out to tell me anything was wrong, I could only assume it wasn't his emergency.

After what seemed to be an eternity, my name was finally called. While being led into the recovery area to be reunited with my husband, I was told he made it through the surgery and was now alert.

As I rounded the corner, I found him relaxing on his gurney, still dressed in his surgical attire, and I was relieved to know he was fine. In order to create some privacy between the recuperating patients, his gurney was currently enclosed by privacy curtains on three sides, which could be opened or closed by sliding the curtains along the supports that ran along the top. He was smiling and chatting with the nurses and aides on duty, just passing time until he received further instructions.

When I reached his side, I picked up his hand and held it in mine. The minute he looked at me, I saw an uncertainty in his expression that didn't match the optimistic chatter I heard when I first walked in.

There wasn't time to verbalize my observation because the nurse suddenly said it was time for my husband to dress, in preparation for our post-operative meeting discussion with the doctor. Trying to be helpful, I closed all of the curtains around us and handed him his clothing, and then his boots, one piece at a time.

Once he was dressed, an aide brought us to a private area in the recovery room and instructed us to take a seat. She said the doctor would be with us shortly.

My heart sank when the doctor finally came into view for the look on his face was grim. As he approached, I prepared myself for bad news, even though all morning long I had prayed for positive results.

Fearing my husband would sense the anxiety building up inside of me, as a precaution, I didn't look at him. Instead, I just stared at the doctor and waited for him to speak.

Without hesitation, the doctor got right to the point. He told us that he had put a rush on the results and hoped to have them in a few days. My heart sank when his voice became grave, and he proceeded to say, "My views were excellent, and I have been doing this for a long time . . . "

I lost control and began to cry when he looked directly at my husband and said, "I am sorry, but in my educated opinion the appearance and color of the tumor is indicative of cancer. Although I need to get the cytology report to confirm, I am 99% sure you have cancer."

Searching for some ray of hope while the tears ran down my face, my inquiry was more pleading than questioning when I asked if there was any chance the results might indicate the mass had not progressed to the point of a positive cancer result and might possibly still be at a pre-cancerous stage?

Not wanting to unrealistically raise our hopes, the doctor replied, "There is always a chance, but I am not optimistic."

He wasn't cold-hearted in his revelation. There was compassion in his voice throughout our conversation. After all, there was no easy way to break this type of news to a patient.

Because proper nutrition was going to play an important role in my husband's ability to maintain his strength and endurance during treatment, I wanted to know if the doctor might have seen some form of obstruction during the endoscopy, which might explain the escalating swallowing problems he had recently started to experience. Since my husband didn't have time to discuss this particular issue with the oncologist at length during his last visit to the Providence VA, we needed to know if his Parkinson's disease might be the cause for his swallowing disorder in the event no obstruction was present.

The doctor verified that he saw no reason for my husband's tumor to cause his swallowing disorder, because he said his view was clear and my husband's esophagus was unobstructed. Although the doctor stated that Parkinson's disease wasn't his specialty, he suggested we pursue the Parkinson's theory in our attempt to find a solution for this ailment.

In my final attempt to find a sliver of hope in our current predicament, I questioned whether stomach cancer would be easier to cure than pancreatic cancer since my husband's tumor appeared to be located in the lining between the stomach and the pancreatic wall, and its origin had not yet been determined.

I could tell our unfolding tragedy affected the doctor because now his grim look turned into a sad one when he replied, "I am sorry to say, in your husband's case, neither one would be preferable to the other."

As he turned to walk down the hall, to attend to his next scheduled appointment, the doctor apologetically said, "I wish you both the best."

During our ride home, there wasn't much we said to each other, but I was amazed to note that my husband and I still found optimism in our current situation.

For now, we still hoped the results would indicate a pre-cancerous status.

CHAPTER 13

Life Becomes A See-Saw Ride

A positive cancer diagnosis was confirmed five days after the biopsy procedure was performed, and an appointment was immediately scheduled with an oncology doctor at the Providence VA for the Tuesday following the test results. This meant it took eleven days for the test to be completed, the results to be processed, and a follow-up appointment to take place. Considering the fact that Memorial Day Weekend also ate into this timeframe, we were extremely pleased with the scheduling process.

On the day before the oncology doctor's scheduled meeting, my husband received a call from one of the nurses in the oncology department. Unbeknownst to us, behind the scene, an arrangement was being made for my husband to meet with a surgical cancer specialist at the VA Hospital located in West Roxbury, MA, to determine if he could possibly be a candidate for surgery.

The surgeon's staff reported they had an opening for Tuesday, the same day my husband was scheduled to meet with the oncology doctor at the VA Medical Center's Providence location. If my husband was unavailable, it would be two weeks before the surgeon would be back at the West Roxbury location for his next open appointment date.

At first, my husband was hesitant to accept. He was apprehensive, because if surgery were an option, the surgery would take place in the West Roxbury VA Hospital located just outside of Boston. My husband worried about how long he would have to remain in the hospital, and how would I be able to travel that far a distance alone, in order to be with him every day?

I challenged his concerns and told him we needed to make the appointment first, to find out what treatment options were available, adding, we would work out the details once we knew whether or not he qualified. Most importantly, I stressed that he needed the option on the table first, before he had to make any final decision.

At that time, we didn't know what the surgery entailed, or what his chances for survival would be in the event surgery might be a possibility. I emphasized, he should stop worrying about how difficult the process would be on me and start thinking about what needed to be done to save his life! It didn't take long for me to reason with him, before he reluctantly agreed to accept the appointment.

Had fate finally given us a break by offering encouraging treatment on the horizon? After all, we had no reason to believe his cancer had spread, particularly since two of his biopsy results were inconclusive, even though the third one had finally confirmed his cancer diagnosis. All we could do was hold onto hope that his illness was still in its early stages. Against all odds, we chose to remain optimistic.

It was a long drive to Boston. New England's highways are somewhat obsolete, and backups are common, especially during rush hour. In the event we hit heavy commuter traffic, we allowed three hours travel time.

All VA hospitals are busy places, particularly early in the morning, so when we arrived at the West Roxbury VA Hospital, most of the spots in the lot were already taken. In order to find an open parking space, we had to drive around for a few minutes, but it wasn't long before one became available.

From the outside, the hospital was very impressive. I felt anxious as we walked from the car to the front entrance. Upon entering the building, a two-story mezzanine welcomed us.

Given the fact that excellent directions were provided, we had no problem locating the proper check-in desk in the registration area. Once my husband signed in for his appointment, we sat down to wait our turn. His name was called shortly thereafter, and we were led down the hall, around a corner, to an examination room consisting of a single bed, a desk, as well as a computer and chair for the doctor to record his findings. We were seated and told it would be a few minutes before the doctor would be available.

When we met the doctor, he was very pleasant. After introducing himself, he gave us a quick overview for the reason we were there. He explained that pancreatic cancer might be operable under certain circumstances, but conditions needed to be met before a patient actually qualified for this type of elected surgery. The doctor then said he needed to examine my husband before he discussed the details.

The examination was simple and consisted of the standard scrutiny a patient would undergo at a yearly check-up. I believe it was intended to try to determine my husband's current physical condition to make sure he didn't already appear to be in the final stages of his disease.

With the preliminary exam behind him, we were surprised when the doctor stated he had expected my husband to be in worse physical condition than he appeared. He actually said that my husband didn't look drawn, like most cancer patients do when he meets them at an initial consultation. We found encouragement in the doctor's observations, which led us to believe we might have caught the disease in its early stages.

Following these preliminary discussions, the doctor began to delve into the possible option of surgery, which took us down an alarming path with gloomy survival rates for this specific type of operation. If given the opportunity, the statistics indicated there was a 5% chance of surviving the operation. To make matters worse, only about 5% of those who survived would live for up to a year thereafter. The final unsettling news suggested that in most cases the surgery only extended a patient's life by a matter of a few months, at most.

In the event my husband miraculously qualified, the operation in and of itself would be extensive. The surgical procedure would entail the removal of his spleen, a good portion of his stomach, part of his pancreas and the reattachment of his esophagus. The cut would start at the bottom of his ribcage and end below his stomach.

Of course, the carrot was also dangled in front of us that there was a small percentage of patients who were cured by the process. The odds weren't good, but we were willing to listen.

If surgery were an option, my husband would have to endure chemotherapy first, in order to kill off any free-radical cancer cells which usually cause the cancer to spread. Obviously, even if he were one of the few patients who showed signs of an extended recovery, there was no guarantee the cancer wouldn't metastasize after surviving the operation.

The discouraging news wasn't what we expected. I wondered, if the survival rate for surgery was so low and limiting in its potential to extend the patient's life, why would anyone choose this treatment? On the other hand, when a patient did nothing, the alternative was death.

No matter how poor his chances were, when push came to shove, if he wasn't a candidate for surgery, an extended life expectancy wouldn't be possible.

The doctor noted, considering his diagnosis, my husband's blood count appeared relatively good, and he was optimistic that my husband might qualify.

We were informed that a group of physicians met bi-monthly at this hospital to discuss each patient's prognosis and treatment options. The doctor needed to confirm that my husband's cancer hadn't spread before they would approve him for surgical treatment. A PET scan needed to be performed and reviewed to ascertain his current condition.

After our overload of statistical and depressing probabilities, the doctor gave us a few minutes to allow my husband time to consider the limited options he faced.

Once we were alone, we also discussed how his swallowing problem would enter into the mix. We were extremely concerned that his eating disability would interfere with chemotherapy treatment. If my husband couldn't swallow, how would he be able to fight the side effects of the cancer drugs nutritionally? It was a deplorable situation to be in. Since we only had a few minutes to absorb the alarming information before the doctor returned for the verdict, my husband rationalized his decision to order a PET scan based upon his need to know all of the facts, so we could plan accordingly. Our conversation wasn't easy, but neither were his choices.

A few minutes later when the doctor returned, he was pleased to hear my husband's decision. The doctor said my husband would be contacted within a few days to advise him of the time and place where the PET scan would be performed. He then shook my husband's hand and left to meet his next scheduled patient.

When we left the hospital for our long ride home, during our drive, we discussed the importance of remaining optimistic. We now based our hope, that my husband's cancer hadn't spread, upon the doctor's positive remarks. We were encouraged to think that maybe we would have extra time to be together, possibly longer than we had been led to believe.

Life was becoming a sea-saw ride because our emotions were in a constant state of turmoil. So far, for each upbeat episode we experienced, a downward spiral followed. Thank God we were in this together!

CHAPTER 14

The Countdown Begins

Life becomes complicated once you are diagnosed with cancer. Everything you liked to do, everything you once found to be an integral part of your normal existence is now put on hold. You are faced with a frantic attempt to unravel the secrets which just brought you to this juncture; a bewildering mystery, which caused your body to turn on itself in a suicidal attempt to self-destruct your very existence. It makes no sense!

Yet, this was where we found ourselves, just 18 days after my husband had been released from the hospital with a diagnosis of terminal pancreatic cancer.

One appointment after another had been scheduled. The doctors attempted to travel through a maze of medical information and test results to determine my husband's options, during which time, we continued to hope some miracle was possible to save his life or, at the very least, extend it. Unfortunately, every precious day on the road was a countdown in his life.

Considering the fact, previously stated, that Memorial Day Weekend had cut into the limited appointment openings which were available upon such short notice, the speed at which his ultrasound, biopsy procedure, cytology report, and surgeon's interview took place, was truly remarkable.

It was already Wednesday, June 3rd. It had only been one day since my husband's interview with the surgeon, and his first appointment with the head oncology doctor at the Providence VA was about to take place.

Our morning started off optimistically, with hopeful anticipation of a satisfactory result from the soon to be scheduled PET scan, which enabled us to engage in a pleasant conversation as we headed to the VA. Our upbeat exchanges were the way we stayed positive in our never-ending joint attempts to remain optimistic.

As we rode along, I remember asking, "If given a choice, would you consider undergoing an operation?"

I could tell by the swiftness of my husband's response that this thought had been heavy on his mind because he snipped, "I haven't made up my mind yet, since I'm not certain the benefits outweigh the risks."

All I could say out loud was, "I understand."

Being selfish, I wanted him to do everything he could to stay alive, even if it meant we would only share one additional minute together.

On the other hand, I struggled with the knowledge that the risks involved could result in his dying on the operating table as well.

The choices were far from perfect.

For a second, my mind drifted off into my own little world, where I didn't share my negative thoughts with my husband. The silence which followed my question led me to believe he wasn't pleased with the direction our current conversation was heading, because the tone in his voice had suddenly changed.

Before I made matters worse, I realized the time had come to concentrate on happier thoughts. Besides, the stress of his limited options had affected my attitude as well.

In an attempt to improve both of our dispositions, I decided to turn the Sirius XM radio to a comedy station, and it worked. The outlandishness of some of the jokes helped take our minds off his circumstances and suddenly, we were able to laugh again.

When we arrived at the VA for his appointment, our wait to see the doctor was brief, as usual. The long delays of years ago no longer plagued the Providence VA, at least not as far as our experiences were concerned. Because we didn't have to sit and stress out over the conversation we were about to have with the oncology doctor, our short wait made it easier for us.

Once we were brought into the small examination room, while waiting for our appointment to begin, my husband and I discussed our optimistic thoughts about the reason for today's appointment. We believed the conversation would revolve around the surgeon's positive remarks made during our consultation the day before; and we expected the oncology doctor to offer promising treatment options to fight his disease.

Our discussion was interrupted when a young intern entered the room. He looked nervous, and his voice wasn't positive or as assertive as one would expect if he were a seasoned physician. I assumed he might be anxious due to my husband's terminal illness status. I was sure it wasn't easy for even an experienced doctor to deal with the emotional crisis the patient and family were going through.

After the intern introduced himself, he sat down at the computer to update my husband's medical records prior to our conference with the doctor.

The question and answer period was short. He wanted to know if my husband had lost any weight, or were there any new issue which might have arisen since my husband's initial appointment with his primary care doctor?

Since there was nothing new to report, the intern signed off on my husband's case and left us alone to await the doctor's arrival.

It didn't take long before the doctor entered the room. She was accompanied by two social service representatives. Once she introduced herself and her staff, even though the doctor was extremely pleasant, she was all business and got right down to the meat of the matter. There was no sugar coating the situation.

As it turned out, the appointment did not yield the promising outlook we had hoped for. The only information available to discuss at this time was the biopsy report, which had recently confirmed my husband's pancreatic cancer diagnosis. We quickly learned the appointment was intended to provide my husband with the treatment opportunities currently on the table. She presented the hard facts my husband now faced, as well as his odds for survival, and the news wasn't encouraging.

There was no easy way to say it. The doctor confirmed what we had previously been told during his hospital stay. The length of time he had left to live wouldn't exceed six months to a year.

The doctor suggested, "Even if you are a candidate for an operation, provided your cancer hasn't spread, there are serious risks involved. Chemotherapy is the only other option available, but you need to understand, chemo alone will not extend your life more than a month or two, if at all."

We had come to the appointment with hopes my husband's cancer might be treatable. Instead, we had been given grim statistics which pertained to his bleak outlook. As her pessimistic words sank in, our optimism quickly evaporated.

In addition to the discouraging options the doctor proposed, she also explained that treatment meant routine appointments, chemotherapy, possible surgery, blood work, as well as other forms of cancer therapy, which would take up his valuable time, until death stopped the cycle.

This was the moment when the doctor finally said, "Most pancreatic cancer patients opt for no treatment at all. Should you select this option, all treatment would cease through the VA system. You would be turned over to Hospice care, covered through Medicare, and allowed to die with dignity."

When the hopelessness of our situation had been brought out into the open, we soon realized there would be no ray of sunshine to mask the darkness of the situation. I can't begin to explain how devastated I felt. This was the first time the impact of the word terminal hit its mark.

I tried my best but could no longer hold back the tears I had bottled up since the beginning of our conversation. The doctor comforted me and said, "It's okay to cry."

Meanwhile, my husband sat rigid and speechless. He displayed no emotion at all. His willpower amazed me. In the face of death, his resolve seemed unbroken. How I wish I knew what was going through his mind, so that I could tap into his strength.

Before the appointment ended, my husband said he still wanted to know the results of a PET scan. He asked the doctor to find out if one had been scheduled as of yet, because he wouldn't make a decision until after the results were in.

The doctor told us the full body PET/CT scan had been scheduled for June 11th, which meant an eight-day wait from that day. I now wondered, what percentage of the time he had left would be eaten up during this period?

CHAPTER 15

Pretending Life Was Normal

Back on the home front, my sister and her husband were relentless in their attack on the problem at hand. They worked feverishly trying to find any information which might be helpful to combat my husband's disease, especially when it came to medical studies which might shed some light on what we were up against.

Due to the fact my husband's appointments consumed so much of our time and energy, processing all of the information they provided became overpowering. I actually reached a point when I had to tell them to stop their research for a while.

Sometimes it became necessary to force myself to become emotionally detached, because it was heartbreaking to read all of the medical documentation their searches generated. When I thought about the well-defined mortality rates, which were explicitly detailed throughout each paper, it became too painful . . . for those statistics referred to his chances for survival as well.

At times, I found it easier to deal with his illness when I pretended he wasn't sick and our life was normal. I believe we both shared this fantasy, in-between appointments, when we tried to relax.

Once my husband started to feel a little stronger, we made a point to get on with our lives without walking on eggshells every minute of the day. He didn't want to live the remainder of his life that way.

As spring transitioned into the start of early summer, the budding trees were now in bloom. The crocus, tulips, day lilies and lavender had flowered, along with the phlox. This time of year had always been inspiring since we enjoyed watching the fruits of our labor blossom into such beauty.

This year's warm spring breezes brought early buds to the cascading roses, with their sweet aroma permeating throughout our fenced English garden where they grew. As the once beautiful rose pedals withered before my eyes, lost their scent and fell to the ground, it reminded me of how swiftly time was passing.

I was not only saddened at the thought that this could be the last year we would enjoy the beauty of nature's revival together, I was distraught at the idea of possibly being alone the next time the flowers came into bloom.

Nature's spring cycle had completed its journey for yet another year. As much as I desired it, there was no power on earth to stop the march of time as precious minutes were ticking away.

So, I made it my mission to prove the pessimistic doctors' timetable wrong.

We hadn't been told there was no hope, at least not yet. But, since time was of the essence, we needed to follow up on some of the extensive information gathered by our support team: my sister, her husband and our daughter.

Part of the research they gathered uncovered non-traditional methods of treatment, which weren't intended to be implemented as a stand-alone cure, but were meant to be utilized simultaneously with standard cancer treatment plans. So, we decided to further explore natural remedies which have existed for ages.

In olden days, items such as herbs, berries, and even tree bark, which grew naturally in the wild, were harvested. They were used to treat different ailments before modern-day pharmaceuticals became the improved alternative. Since we were quickly running out of options, the time had come to look outside of the box and enlist the aid of the specialists in the field of natural medicine still being practiced today.

We hadn't gone down this rabbit hole earlier because we knew standard cancer treatment was the most effective method available to provide a cure, but it didn't have to be the only line of defense used to deliver health benefits. The only natural approach we had incorporated thus far included the addition of organic vegetables, foods and homeopathic remedies to enhance nutritional benefits.

The time had come to meet with a doctor who specialized in natural medicine, who would work alongside the oncology doctors to fight my husband's battle against his diseases. Therefore, while we waited for the PET scan to be performed, I researched online to find a local naturopathic physician who might be able to assist with nutritional and homeopathic remedies we hoped would extend my husband's life.

As luck would have it, there was a well-qualified naturopathic physician in our area who was also the Dean of the College of Naturopathic Medicine at the University of Bridgeport. Upon further investigation, I discovered treatment was open to the public, provided it concurred with the medical education being offered at the university.

I was surprised when, on my very first try, I reached the Dean herself. After I described my husband's situation, she sympathetically explained that it was necessary for her to review my husband's case prior to scheduling an appointment. She understood the severity of his illness and promised she would rush her review once I provided the medical documentation she needed to evaluate their ability to help.

As promised, the Dean's response was quick and resulted in a conference being scheduled for the following Tuesday, June 9th.

We were pleased to tell my sister and her husband about our new plan of attack. When they offered to come along, we thought their extensive knowledge could be helpful, and we appreciated any additional information they might bring to the table.

Time was flying by, and before we knew it, our appointment day was upon us. Since it was our first meeting and Bridgeport wasn't our normal stomping grounds, we weren't exactly sure where the medical building was located on the university campus. In order to avoid the heavy traffic which could cause us to miss our appointment, we started out earlier than normal. Luckily, when we arrived, we had no problem finding the appropriate building, along with a parking spot within a short walking distance thereof. When we approached the entrance, I took a deep breath and hoped some miracle might lie behind the massive metal and glass doors, which led to the reception area.

As we entered the building, my nerves were in turmoil. I felt tension in my chest, similar to what a student might feel in anticipation of a final exam. I accompanied my husband to the reception desk, and then we sat down next to each other while I quietly filled out the paperwork he had been given.

My husband carried on a light-hearted conversation with my sister and brother-in-law, who were seated nearby. His spirits were up, while I silently worried what we would do next if this appointment didn't pan out. This thought now weighed heavily on my mind.

When my husband tried to draw me into their conversation, he picked up on the fact that my silence wasn't the result of my preoccupation with his paperwork. He knew me too well. He understood, when I was quiet, something was wrong, and he was correct in his assumption. At the moment, I wasn't only worried, I was desperate for good news.

For his sake, I always tried to put on an act of confidence, but today just happened to be one of those days when my husband caught me off guard.

Suddenly, I realized my solemn mood had affected his positive outlook because a negative transformation, from his previous cheerful disposition, took place without warning. It was as though I had flipped a switch, which suddenly caused his lighthearted demeanor to dissolve into an aura of gloom, and it was up to me to turn the situation around.

To reboot my husband's spousal support system, I carefully tucked away my fears and shifted my negative vibes into positive ones. Being the happy one, the one who never got upset, made it easy for me to snap him out of a bad mood I might have caused, by changing the subject and engaging him in a cheerful conversation. When he sensed my brightened tone, we both benefited. I had learned early on in our relationship, that it was easier to deal with negative situations through positive interactions. It was just that now, under the current circumstances, it was extremely difficult to be in an up mood all the time because I feared the difficult road ahead.

Shortly after obtaining my objective of improving my husband's temperament, a pretty young intern introduced herself and instructed us to follow her to the meeting location for our scheduled appointment. Following a short elevator ride, we walked down a brightly lit hallway until we reached the conference room door on the right. We were all ushered in and told it would just be a few minutes before our consultation with the Dean and members of her staff would take place.

The conference room wasn't much different than you would expect to find in a standard office building complex, except for the stunning million-dollar view of Long Island Sound. To make light of the situation, once our medical team entered, my husband started his normal trivial chit-chat, questioning how the university was able to afford such a view.

Following a minute or two of similar small talk, our conversation settled into the main reason for our visit and what we hoped to accomplish.

Before she asked my husband to provide any additional information he felt might be important, the Dean explained my husband's case history to her team. My husband filled in the blanks by including the fact that his cancer had not been staged as of yet, and a PET scan was scheduled to take place two days from that day. He completed his contribution of information by explaining that chemotherapy, followed by surgery, would be offered through the VA provided his cancer had not spread. Should the PET scan indicate his cancer had metastasized, chemotherapy alone, or a non-treatment hospice plan was the only other alternative the VA had to offer.

Everyone in the room knew my husband's case was terminal. It was just a matter of when he would die, not if. Therefore, when the Dean asked my husband what he hoped to achieve through their intervention, his main objective was to improve his swallowing difficulties, so he could eat normally and meet his nutritional needs.

It was a simple enough request. Unfortunately, his eating disorder had deteriorated to the point that it had become problematic. On top of all the other problems he faced, if there was no remedy, he would starve to death before he died from his cancer.

The university doctors agreed that Parkinson's Disease could be the cause of my husband's swallowing issues and a stomach feeding tube might be his only choice as the condition worsened, because there was no other alternative treatment option they were aware of.

Because the VA doctor had suggested the feeding tube option at his last oncology appointment, my husband had already thought it through. It was not a solution he would entertain, no matter how serious the situation became. He told the doctors he didn't want to die tied up to machines or any other artificial paraphernalia.

When we mentioned the organic vegetable juicing and fresh soups I had already incorporated into his diet, the Dean agreed that it was crucial for him to maintain his weight, which was a fundamental aspect in his battle against the disease.

Before the university team left the room for a private consultation, they reviewed all of the organic foods, vitamins, supplements and detox teas my sister and her husband had recommended. They then suggested the ones my husband should continue to take for nutritional values and anti-cancer potentials.

Upon their return, we were led to believe helpful recommendations could be provided to address the negative side effects of my husband's cancer treatment, should he choose that route. The Dean encouragingly mentioned, the team had successfully dealt with other cancer patients who had undergone chemotherapy with good results. In our desperate situation, her account provided hope.

On the side of caution, she wanted to be certain we understood that pancreatic cancer wasn't curable because she didn't want us to be unrealistic in our expectations. On a positive note, she believed if my husband got proper nutrients through his continued effort to eat smaller meals throughout the day, and he took part in the VA cancer treatment options available, he stood a good chance of increasing his odds to extend his life.

So, at this particular moment, things looked more promising than we had anticipated.

Another appointment was scheduled for June 30th to discuss the PET scan results and the medical treatment choices available to my husband should chemotherapy, proceeded by surgery, be an option. If so, the university's medical team would be able to provide him with a subordinate plan to coincide with this type of treatment.

Even though my husband wasn't certain he would undergo surgery, if given the option, we needed the encouragement this appointment provided. But, as we left, I wondered if the benefit of the doctors' inspiring words would be short lived ~ or not?

CHAPTER 16

Waiting for Answers

The PET scan, which was needed to further evaluate my husband's options to treat his pancreatic carcinoma diagnosis, took place at the VA Hospital in West Haven, CT on June 11th. The results were crucial to determine whether or not his cancer had spread. If the cancer had metastasized, his options were limited.

Once the scan was completed, he was told it would take a few days for the results to filter through the proper VA channels. Therefore, we needed to find some form of enjoyment to help get us through the stressful wait and not dwell upon the life and death scenario currently playing out its hand. Because we always managed to find contentment while on the road, we decided to start taking the potential risk of getting out of the house more often, simply for a change of scenery.

Less than a month earlier, the day before my husband had been admitted to the local hospital, we had just traded in his older convertible sports car for a shiny new maroon one with a beautiful tan interior. Although his older SL was only used during good weather and it had very low mileage, the GPS technology was obsolete and couldn't be brought up to date. We also worried about the cost of repairs, in the event the retractable convertible hard top roof malfunctioned, since we had experienced minor issues with the top already.

Maintenance can be very expensive on foreign cars, and our older convertible had been out of warranty for a few years now. So, we justified our decision to buy the new car based upon safety issues because the older any vehicle becomes, the higher the probability it will break down, usually at very inconvenient times or places. The icing on the cake was that our new purchase came with maintenance coverage, which alleviated our worries about the cost of repairs during the new car warranty period.

We both knew we didn't need a new car, but our decision was a bucket-list choice, which brought joy into our lives. Since my husband had already been diagnosed with Parkinson's disease, I couldn't be certain how much longer he would be able to enjoy his favorite activity, which was driving. I wanted him to relish life while he was still able, especially since at the time we purchased the vehicle, we had no idea he had cancer.

On the day he was released from the hospital, four days after we had purchased the car, my husband told me he wanted to sell his new convertible, but I wouldn't hear of it. I said there was plenty of time to make that decision at a later date. For now, I wanted the car to be our escape from reality. It was a form of mental health . . . medication . . . on wheels. That was a decision I never regretted.

Outwardly, my husband still looked healthy. However, his medical condition wouldn't improve because there was no promising treatment option available to slow down the advancement of his cancer. Due to the dismal cancer survival rate statistics, neither one of us wanted to discuss where our lives were really headed. We were in a waiting game and continuously hoped good news might be right around the corner.

In order to take our minds off his upcoming PET scan results, or any of the other disheartening situations we were dealing with, whenever he suggested a short ride, I was all for it. Only now, instead of planning a stop at a local restaurant to coincide with our outing, I packed a small lunch to take with us. This way, hopefully, he would eat his sandwich in small portions . . . just like the doctor ordered.

Summer was just beginning, and the day's chilly spring air had made a transition into pleasant sunny skies, with a hint of the hot days to come. It was a beautiful day for a drive in a convertible.

While we drove to the New London shoreline, which was the roundabout way to get to the Mystic Seaport area, we stopped to eat our lunch and enjoy the views at numerous picturesque locations we knew along our way. This pleasant pastime became a staple we enjoyed while he was still able to drive.

As I think back during those excursions, it wasn't the beauty of the scenery that comes to mind . . . it was my concern about how little he actually ate. Throughout our drive, I continuously offered him portions of his uneaten sandwich, in order to maintain his weight. He needed more than the few morsels of food he could manage to get down during a single sitting. Despite the fact he tried his best to follow the doctor's eating plan, we both understood his problem went much further than his inability to consume a full meal in one sitting. There just didn't seem to be a viable solution available to solve his swallowing disorder, which doesn't affect every Parkinson's patient.

Admirably, my husband tried his best to live his life as though he was still healthy. He refused to dwell in self-pity, even though he was extremely ill. I believe emotionally, he held up much better than me. If not, he sure put on a good show.

Nowadays, he got exhausted quicker, so our road trips no longer consisted of the all-day excursions of the past. Therefore, when my husband became tired, we returned home and relaxed on our front porch, enjoying the warmth of the summer-like breezes, as we watched our family of humming birds travel past us. I found it fascinating to observe these small delicate creatures, accentuated in their silvery green or brown feathers, as they closely whizzed by, completely unaffected by our presence. It was so sweet when, occasionally, we would see them stop mid-flight in front of us, as though they paused to stare at us as they traveled along their journey in search of their favorite nectar.

I often wondered if they knew the person who dutifully provided the sweet red liquid they so thoroughly enjoyed. Whenever my husband approached the feeder, they moved only a foot or so away, to allow him to refill their favorite delicacy. When he could no longer perform this duty, I discovered that I wasn't permitted the same consideration. Even though I worked at it, I was never able to gain their same level of trust.

During this time, there were many days my sister and brother-in-law stopped by to visit and cheer us up. Most often, weather permitting, they found us on the porch, with our faithful dogs by our side.

We always got along throughout the years, and their visits were always interesting, upbeat, and never boring. An intended short stay, just to check in and say hi, usually took up the whole afternoon.

My sister and her husband weren't dog people. In fact, they were definitely cat people, who shared their home with perky felines during their many years of marriage. I would jokingly say that maybe this explained why their political persuasion could be so different from ours.

In time, our dogs also benefited from their visits. Since my husband's energy had started to dwindle, when my sister and brother-in-law sat down to relax and enjoy a leisurely conversation, suddenly a toy would appear at their feet with a wet nose nudging the toy invitingly to play. It didn't take long before they both began to play the fetch game because my sister and her husband were now hooked by the looks on the loveable, furry faces of our loyal companions.

Soon the dogs learned the sound of their car as it came down the driveway, and they would grab a toy and run to meet them. Not too long thereafter, new toys would show up which caused squeals of joy and excitement from our friendly pack of canines.

It was delightful to watch the attachment grow during their visits. The affection was mutual, as the tit for tat between them became a valuable source of cheerfulness in an otherwise somber setting.

My sister and her husband weren't self-employed like us. Instead, they were both previously employed in management positions at a local casino. Needless to say, when one is on salary, there is no such thing as a 40-hour week. It wasn't until we were all retired, when we actually had time to sit down and compare notes, at which time we were amazed to discover how similar our ideologies really were.

Admittedly, my husband's illness played an important role in our lives because it divulged a better understanding of what family really meant.

When times were trying, there were those who stepped forward and looked for nothing in return. They are the ones who made the heartaches and sorrow bearable, because you knew they cared.

During such periods, no matter whether you win or lose the battle, the ones who walk alongside you and share your pain are the light and strength God sends to help you endure His will.

My account can only begin to attempt to explain how very blessed we both felt to have experienced the thoughtfulness and kindness my sister and brother-in-law brought into our lives when we needed it most.

Diversions like theirs are what it took to get us through the many trials and tribulations we had to undergo throughout his illness. In time we discovered that the secret of enduring our agonizing journey was to hold onto hope, accept the help of others, and believe in God, for He will never cause you to withstand more than you can bear.

CHAPTER 17

Very Poor Odds

D uring the two-week timeframe that it would take for the PET scan to be scheduled and performed, I feared the worst each time I thought about the answer to the key question, had his cancer spread?

Anticipation of the results worried me because I understood good news didn't necessarily equate to a positive outcome. Therefore, I didn't share my doubts with my husband since he had enough on his mind. I could see no point having him anguish over my concerns for I had already worried enough for the both of us.

Early on, while my husband underwent his VA diagnostic testing, the constant barrage of appointments built up our hopes for an optimistic outcome.

Now that our worst fears were confirmed, and we learned his cancer was terminal, to say life became challenging was an understatement.

Yet, throughout the entire process, we felt as though my husband's best interest was always put first, and we were forever grateful for the hard work the VA doctors and staff put forth in their concerted efforts to find a viable treatment plan to extend my husband's life.

As the days became weeks and the weeks turned into a month, we were down to the wire because he had arrived at the end of the line as far as his options were concerned. His PET scan result would be the final catalyst to determine his fate.

Even if my husband opted against chemotherapy or surgery, should they become an option, we prayed we would have more time to be together if his cancer hadn't spread.

So against all likelihood of a successful outcome, since the odds weren't in his favor, we did our best to hold onto hope. After all, isn't that what life's all about, beating the odds?

Once we received word an appointment had been scheduled with the surgeon to review the PET scan results, we felt optimistic. We enthusiastically assumed my husband hadn't been told the outcome over the phone, prior to our appointment, because the doctor must have devised a plan of attack and would discuss the proposal with us in person. With a bit of luck, maybe the doctor would divulge the good news we had been praying for.

We had plenty of time to spare when we arrived at the West Roxbury VA Hospital for my husband's appointment on June 23rd. The hard part was not knowing what life had in store but having plenty of time to think about it.

It took awhile before my husband's name was called because we had arrived so early, but as we followed the aide down the corridor I remember thinking, "Have we finally reached the point when we can get a conclusive answer?"

At first, the doctor was with another patient, so we were told it would be a few minutes before he met with us.

When the doctor finally entered the room, his greeting was warm. He asked my husband how he was feeling in order to determine if there were any substantial changes in his condition since our last visit.

After a few minutes of sociable conversation, the doctor announced, "As a result of the PET scan outcome, your belly button area is a cause for concern. I recommend it be biopsied to determine if your cancer has spread."

My husband had been experiencing discomfort in this region, and more than one doctor had examined the area in question since the start of the whole ordeal, but since cancer of the umbilical area is almost unheard of, his complaint was put on the back burner until his pancreatic cancer diagnosis was hopefully under control. Initially, the doctors believed the issue was minor in comparison to his life-threatening cancer diagnosis; only now, this area had become questionable as well.

Wanting to get the matter resolved as soon as possible and due to the cancer's aggressive nature, the doctor advised, "I can perform the biopsy in my office right now, but it will have to be done without anesthesia, and it will be painful. If you prefer to have it done with anesthesia, we will have to schedule another appointment. Since I am only here every other week, it would be a minimum of a two-week delay, provided I have an opening."

Even though we both were overwhelmed by the doctor's disclosure, we understood the delay would require another trip back to Boston, with an even longer wait period before any results became available.

As I turned away from the doctor to look at my husband, I could tell by his bewildered expression that he needed some time to digest the information. Therefore, I asked the doctor, "Can you please give us a few minutes to talk this over, so my husband can decide what he wants to do?"

The doctor willingly obliged and said he would take care of a few other issues while my husband and I discussed the matter. But, on his way out of the room, he commented, "Because of my schedule, you will have to decide quickly. I don't have much time before my next appointment."

Prior to making this difficult choice, I wanted my husband to think it through. I implored him to consider, "If we reschedule, there will be no pain."

Truer words could not have been spoken, when he replied, "You realize, time is not on my side. We need answers, and I really don't think I have a choice."

Although I understood, he wasn't looking forward to yet another biopsy, I could only nod in agreement. Mindful of the fact that my husband had a high tolerance for pain, I didn't object when he chose to have the biopsy done that day, especially since each delay we encountered only led to more frustration.

When the doctor returned, my husband said he wanted the biopsy done right now, so the doctor took immediate action.

At first, I watched as a large needle was inserted into his naval. His agony became visible in his facial features as his fingers dug into the side of the upholstered mat on the examination table. I had to turn away to avoid seeing the obvious suffering he was experiencing. I respected his courage while he attempted to muffle the sound of the pain he was enduring.

Upon completion of the biopsy, the doctor took the specimen and quickly headed to the pathology department stating, "I want to be certain I have taken a large enough sample to test," as he walked out the door.

Within minutes, he returned with bad news. The tissue was too watery to test and it had fallen apart. Looking directly at my husband, the doctor announced, "If you are up to it, I need to redo the procedure."

I could tell my husband wasn't pleased. It was obvious he didn't want to go through another biopsy, especially now that he was fully aware of the pain involved in the process.

Only this time, there was no hesitation in his decision. With no complaints or harsh words, my husband told the doctor, "Just do it!"

Thinking back, if I were in his position, I don't know if I could have complied. It took unbelievable willpower to go through the excruciating pain all over again.

The next time around, I couldn't watch any of the procedure. Although I averted my gaze, the stifling sounds of my husband's agony disclosed more than I wanted to know.

Thank goodness it didn't take long before the second biopsy was over and the doctor left, specimen in hand, to confirm he had finally acquired an acceptable cell count.

Fortunately, this time when he returned, he was smiling. He announced he had obtained sufficient tissue samples for testing purposes.

Before he left to attend to his next patient, the doctor let us know, "It will take about a week for the results to be available. If the cancer hasn't spread, we will schedule another appointment to discuss your options."

Obviously, the day didn't go as well as we had planned, but then again, I guess life rarely does.

I often thought, if courage alone were the deciding factor in my husband's battle against cancer, things might have turned out differently.

CHAPTER 18

Thoughtful Gifts

The discouraging results of the PET scan, which required the surgeon at the West Roxbury VA to perform another biopsy, made it difficult to keep a positive outlook. Admittedly, the constant dissemination of bad news was taking its toll on our confidence, and most patients, by this point, might have given up hope. However, we still had faith in God, even though it seemed apparent there might not be a light at the end of the tunnel after all.

We tried to keep our conversation positive during our drive home, although considering the circumstances, it was difficult to do. We were struggling to find a cheery common ground to chat about when a phone call interrupted our conversation, as we were maneuvering through heavy traffic outside of the Boston area.

It was my sister. She was aware of our appointment and had hoped for good news. She wanted to know how my husband made out.

Sadly, there was no good news to share. Now that the possibility of the spread of my husband's cancer had been raised, I could barely keep from crying when I reported the PET scan findings to her. "It is just more areas of concern and more waiting," I replied.

Trying to conceal the disappointment in her voice, my sister proceeded to reveal the main reason for her call. She and her husband were on their way to a religious store in Colchester to purchase a scapular medal as a present for my husband. Since we were on the road already, they wanted to know if we were interested in meeting them, so my husband could choose the one he preferred.

Touched by their thoughtfulness, as he listened to the conversation over our car's audio system, my husband nodded his head in agreement. He apologetically replied, it would take at least an hour for us to get there since we were still in MA.

"No problem," she responded. They would take care of other errands to pass the time until we got there. Before we said our goodbyes, we agreed to meet at the religious store parking lot in approximately an hour.

Her call managed to brighten our thoughts and conversation since we now had a positive purpose in mind.

Throughout my husband's illness, God was on our mind A LOT. After my sister called, I commented to my husband about how many times compassionate acts by others seemed to occur in our darkest hour. We both agreed, the Lord knew exactly when we needed His help.

We never questioned the premise that the likelihood of my husband's survival would be based upon God's will; but we believed God supported us in many other ways, such as the simple acts of kindness which were being bestowed upon us. We never felt as though we walked alone through the valley of death.

Now, with faith in our hearts, the time and distance passed quickly. Before long, we arrived at our destination and pulled into the small parking lot.

Since they had reached the tiny store ahead of us, my sister and brother-in-law were already inside, where she had eagerly started her search for the perfect gift. When we entered, my sister couldn't hide her enthusiasm. Their early arrival had given her time to browse in pursuit of her quest, and her search was fruitful. She had located not only one, but many options from which my husband could choose.

Our greeting was warm, as though we hadn't seen each other for ages. As we hugged, her smile was broad and beaming with love, symbolic of a person whose intention was to provide comfort during my husband's time of need. Right away, she led us to the display case, nestled in the back of the store.

Even though she already knew which three she liked best, she didn't want to influence my husband's choice. I understood the importance my sister placed upon my husband's spiritual well-being. Out of the goodness of her heart, she wanted him to have first choice before she and I selected from the remaining collection.

There was no hesitation on my husband's part; his decision was cut and dry. He chose a small silver medallion, scripted with the face of the Sacred Heart of Jesus on the front of the medal and the Blessed Virgin's image on the back.

My sister was especially pleased with his choice since it was the exact one she would have picked had he not felt well enough to come and decide for himself.

On the other hand, during my turn, it took a while before I narrowed down my choice to two, from the many medals on display. Surprisingly, my sister had chosen them as her first and second choice as well.

Knowing I favored the same two medals, due to the circumstances, she insisted I choose first. Upon my decision, my sister delightedly admitted that she had ended up with her favorite choice of them all.

Once our selections were completed, for some unknown reason, I was inspired to purchase a rosary. Since I felt as though I had received a spiritual directive, I moved over to the beautiful rosary beads on display in the adjacent glass showcase. Although I hadn't said the rosary for years, suddenly, I wanted to renew the ritual I had so long ago abandoned.

The choices varied from sparkling crystal beads to the simple wooden design I chose. Even though I knew my prayers were being heard with or without the use of a rosary, I felt comforted as I cupped and cradled the rosary beads within my hands. Unexpectedly, a feeling of contentment warmed my heart. I knew there was no guarantee a rosary would suddenly make everything better, but I believed through its use, I would gain some spiritual strength to accept the inevitable.

Completely satisfied with the selections we made, I walked down the narrow aisle to the old cash register, which sat on top of the end of the showcase. I intended to pay for my portion of the purchases, while off to the side, my husband stood waiting for me.

When the sales lady didn't approach me to transact my purchase, I was surprised. Instead, she walked up to my husband and inquired if he was interested in buying a new rosary as well, to support him along his difficult journey. She appeared to be a caring woman, who knew my husband was ill because my sister had already told her he had terminal cancer.

I was touched by the sincere expression displayed on her face as I overheard their tranquil conversation. A noticeable change overcame her appearance when my husband looked directly at her, with a peaceful expression on his face, and said, "I have a rosary, the one I used a long time ago when I served in Vietnam."

My husband expanded on his comment by explaining that he always kept his rosary nearby, especially during his tours of duty in Vietnam. He drove his point home by stating, he believed the Blessed Virgin's blessings helped bring him home alive. Once he explained his reason for wanting to keep his old rosary, he thanked the woman for her kind offer, and then, for some unknown reason he added, ". . . even though mine is missing a few beads, I will continue to use my old rosary when I pray."

The part about the missing beads was my fault. My husband always kept this particular rosary in the car to protect us while we traveled. One day, a long time ago, while I searched for some long-forgotten item in the glove compartment, a small portion of his rosary somehow got lodged in the bottom crack of the open door.

As I pushed the glove compartment door to close it, I heard a crunch. I knew his favorite rosary was kept there and hoped my suspicions were wrong. Unfortunately, my worst fear was confirmed when I quickly reopened the door to find a few broken wooden beads, which I tenderly picked up in my hands.

At that moment, when I told my husband what I had done, he wasn't angry, although his voice expressed a certain sadness, as though he experienced a personal injury when learning of the unfortunate incident. When I showed him the small, broken pieces, he solemnly said, "Put it back where it belongs."

I could tell the storekeeper was affected by my husband's faith in his rosary because I heard her say she had a gift for him in her car. "Please watch the store for me," she muttered, as she hurried out the front door to retrieve it.

By now, we were all curious. What could be so important that the woman would leave strangers alone in the store unattended?

It only took a minute or two before she returned. Once she reached my husband, she gently placed a rosary into his unexpecting hands. When he looked at her in bewilderment, she whispered, "It's a gift."

While I watched from my location, I saw tears in his eyes. Since his diagnosis, this was the first time I witnessed an emotional response from him. He was speechless and stumbled over his words as he offered to pay her for his precious gift, but she wouldn't hear of it. By now, there wasn't a dry eye amongst us.

She tenderly explained to my husband, this rosary had an extra bead and that was why she knew it was meant for him. During her visit to a little village in Bosnia, known as Medjugorje, she had purchased it, intending to give it to a person in need who might benefit from the Blessed Virgin's intervention.

Shortly thereafter, we paid for our purchase and left the store. Later, we discovered that my sister had picked up the conversation where my husband's exchange had ended. She chatted with the shopkeeper to find out more information about the rosary and its story. My sister learned the shopkeeper had visited Medjugorje a few times in the past, and the woman indicated she had always remembered a feeling of spiritual enrichment during her visits.

The village of Medjugorje is a site where the apparition of the Blessed Virgin Mary is said to be currently appearing, requesting prayers for peace in the world, the conversion of sinners, penance, and daily prayer of the rosary.

The shopkeeper had purchased the rosary approximately 2½ years earlier. She was led to believe the rosary had been blessed during a reported visitation from the Blessed Virgin, as well as by a local priest in that location.

During the past few years, the woman prayed continuously to the Blessed Virgin and asked for guidance to help her decide who Our Lady's planned recipient of the rosary should be. She further explained, she never thought the right person had come along until she met my husband. When she learned from my sister about my husband's story of terminal illness, combined with his own account of the missing beads on his rosary, she now believed he was the planned recipient of Our Lady's intention.

Intrigued by the religious woman's explanation, and intent upon passing on the rest of the emotionally charged account of the story regarding the rosary, my sister immediately called us once she left the store. After learning the whole story behind the rosary's journey, my husband and I thought, although the gift alone was precious, the history behind the rosary's story was priceless!

It was easy to tell my husband was humbled by the experience. He cherished his gift and carried this rosary with him everywhere to use in daily prayer. I believe his gift renewed his devotion to God at an important time in his life. Its use appeared to have helped him achieve an inner peace and reconnection with God on a positive spiritual level, as well as with the Blessed Virgin, who he had always implored to protect him throughout his life.

Although my husband was courageous during his entire ordeal, it seemed to me that he felt extraordinarily blessed by this incident and found the spirituality we somehow mislaid along life's journey. His appreciation of the gift was evident by his insistence that the rosary was not to be buried with him but must continually be passed down to family members after his death.

I have confidence, my husband reclaimed his faith that day through the thoughtful gifts he had received.

CHAPTER 19

Another Door Had Been Closed

The month of June was quickly ending. While we prayed for good news, precious moments of our lives together were slipping away. As I became more aware of the negative side effects my husband's illness was having on his health, it led me to believe he was living on borrowed time unless the doctors were able to provide some form of effective treatment.

As my husband slowly lost weight and his endurance showed signs of decline, my hope that the doctors would find some promising treatment to extend his life was deteriorating at the same time.

No matter how gloomy the prospect of my husband's survival became, we didn't look at life as though we had been dealt a bad hand. Even during the many times when despair took hold, for we weren't exempt from these feelings, we wouldn't allow ourselves to dwell in utter hopelessness. We strove to help each other maintain a positive attitude in order to sustain our fragile support system for each other.

Since my husband's last appointment at the University of Bridgeport, we received the bad news that his PET scan results revealed the possibility his cancer had spread. Now we awaited another biopsy report to either confirm or deny this likelihood.

When we arrived for our June 30th appointment at the university, we were greeted by the same young intern we had met in the lobby at our initial conference. I could tell she had taken a liking to us the last time we were there because of her cheery conversation in the elevator, while we were leaving that day, and the smile on her face today.

Only now, when her smile of recognition was met by my husband's quiet demeanor and lack of a lighthearted conversation, it became blatantly obvious to her that something must be terribly wrong. I noticed a quick modification in her behavior when her happy smile turned into a solemn expression as we followed her to our intended destination.

My husband's current subdued mannerisms were so unlike him. But, when you considered the circumstances, it was totally understandable.

Once our meeting began, my husband addressed the medical team and described the concerns the VA surgeon expressed regarding the numerous hot spots revealed on the PET scan. He informed the team that another biopsy had been performed by the surgeon in order to confirm if his cancer had spread. The fact that the biopsy results weren't available was just a technicality. By this point, we were pretty certain the results would show it already had.

There was a difference in our enthusiasm at this appointment since neither my husband nor I were optimistic any viable options would be available to help extend his life. It was difficult to be cheery when the only investment of hope we counted on, no longer seemed to afford the silver lining we had banked on.

Surgery no longer seemed to be the promising option it once was, and because the team now sensed the negative change in my husband's previous optimistic attitude, we all agreed another appointment wouldn't be necessary unless my husband intended to continue his effort to fight the disease.

Although the doctors were still optimistic they could help him deal with the side effects of chemotherapy treatment, he questioned whether the short-term benefit, if any, was worth the risks, especially since he would be sick and under constant medical treatment until he died.

The discouraging news seemed to affect the doctors as well, because it was obvious they looked disappointed to learn the gloomy information no one had anticipated.

To keep on track and professional, the doctors continued to stress the important role nutrition played in my husband's struggle to survive. This was a tall order because his swallowing problem had continued its downward spiral. I assumed that the Dean perceived the hopelessness of our situation, because it appeared as though she had searched for a needle in the haystack in her effort to provide us with some encouragement. Since they had already recommended their treatment options, she suggested my husband schedule an appointment with a homeopathic doctor, who might provide a natural remedy for his eating disorder. Uncertain if we would travel down this path, but grateful for her thoughtfulness, I wrote down the names of both the doctors she recommended before we left the conference area.

At this juncture, my husband was overwhelmed and unprepared to take on any new approaches before learning the biopsy results. Knowing his lifespan was limited, I could only assume what was going through his mind. It was obvious he was troubled, undecided if his fight was over since the most important part of the puzzle was still missing. At the moment, he had no direction or course to follow.

At the end of our appointment, the young intern led us back down the hall. Then, during our ride in the elevator, it surprised us to hear the sincerity in her voice when she said how impressed she was by our obvious love for each other. She was very sorry to hear my husband wasn't doing well, and she hoped there was more that could be done to help him. When the elevator doors opened on the main level, she shook our hands and wished us luck before we walked out into the hall. A look of sadness showed in her eyes as the elevator doors closed and she headed back upstairs to return to her studies.

We walked away with the feeling that another door had now been closed in our search for a plausible treatment plan, or alternative to extend my husband's life. The fact that life would continue on for everyone else, while ours was coming to an end, never felt as real as it did at that moment.

CHAPTER 20

A Path To Follow

On the 1st of July, we received a call from the surgeon's office at the West Roxbury VA Hospital. When I answered the phone, I was told the doctor wanted to speak with my husband if he was available.

Understanding the implication, my husband was hesitant to take the call, although he was aware the doctor would only speak to him to discuss the PET scan results. We were on the road at the time, so my husband pulled the car into a lot, parked it, and reached for the phone because he didn't want to postpone the inevitable.

Once the nurse confirmed my husband was on the phone, the doctor got on the line to reveal the biopsy results. He told my husband they were positive, which meant his cancer had spread. Therefore, my husband wouldn't be eligible for surgery, and chemotherapy, though not a stand-alone treatment, would be the only medical option available. When the doctor asked if my husband had any questions, he replied, "No, I'm all set. Thank you for the information."

Even though we anticipated the possibility of this outcome, neither one of us had prepared ourselves to actually hear or acknowledge the phrase, your cancer has spread; nor were we ready to accept the consequences of the significance of the results.

I didn't have to ask what the doctor said because I already knew the news wasn't good by the tone of my husband's voice when he responded to the doctor.

My husband was devastated. Although he didn't break down, his eyes glazed over, and a blank stare overtook the relaxed expression which had existed just minutes earlier.

As we sat in silence, I searched for words of comfort, but found none. I was as distraught as he was, and all I could do was reach over and take his hand in mine.

This time, his response was strikingly different because the verdict was in, and we had reached the end of the line. For the first time, he let me see his despair. With a look of hopelessness on his face and in a monotone voice, he said, "It's over."

I knew exactly how he felt. Not only was his life over . . . so was mine!

Granted, I was overwhelmed as well, but my sadness was insignificant to his anguish. I became desperate to help him deal with his fatal disclosure.

Even though I didn't have a plan, I wanted him to believe we still had hope, so I told him it wasn't over yet.

Unexpectedly, he called my bluff and asked, "What is there left to do?"

Now, I was stuck. I needed something positive to say . . . and then it came to me. Although it represented only a small chance for an encouraging outcome, I said, "We are going to make an appointment with one of the naturopathic doctors the university suggested at our last appointment. Even though they may not have a cure, one of the doctors may have a solution to your eating disorder, which might give you more time."

The idea presented a spark of optimism. Immediately, a glimmer of hope, which hadn't been there a second ago, appeared in his eyes.

He asked me, "Do you really think it will help?"

I smiled and said, "Of course it will. After all, we have nothing to lose."

Even though my suggestion offered only a slim chance for a successful outcome, the solution led to another roadblock. We were now approaching the 4th of July weekend, and I wondered how long it would take to get an appointment.

Since I already had the doctors' names and both came highly recommended, we decided to call both offices. We would schedule an appointment with whoever could offer the earliest possible date.

I couldn't control the shaking of my hands as I looked up the phone numbers on my iPhone and started making the calls.

My voice cracked during my stressful conversations, while I spoke to the office assistant at each firm and tried to explain the urgency in my husband's need for an appointment. Both women were extremely sympathetic, but each one told me the normal wait period for an appointment would be between four to six weeks. Both comfortingly added, they would speak with their doctor to determine if an earlier appointment could be scheduled. They each promised to reply as soon as possible, but I knew there was no guarantee either call would come through before the end of the day.

Neither my husband, nor I, lost faith in humanity that day, for I believe the goodness which exists in people exceeds the sorrows we are meant to suffer. I say this because we were amazed that it only took a few minutes before we received our first call back, although later that afternoon, we heard from the other office assistant as well.

Despite the fact that the call came quickly, my heart sank when the office assistant told us the doctor was leaving for a conference in Europe at the beginning of the following week. What she said next, astonished us both.

The caring woman said their office would be closed for the weekend, starting on Friday, July 3rd, in observation of the 4th of July holiday. If we were available to come in on the 3rd, the doctor offered to meet with us, even though he had no office hours scheduled for that day.

Amazed and extremely grateful, we jumped at the opportunity. "Of course we'll come," I replied. After all, this meant the appointment would take place in a day and a half, instead of a month. We were both shocked at the doctor's compassion.

Needless to say, there was a caveat. The assistant's vacation was scheduled to start on Thursday the 2nd, and today was Wednesday the 1st. In order to schedule the appointment for Friday the 3rd, I needed to fax a completed new patient application, which she would email me, along with my husband's medical history before she left the office at the end of the day. Without the completed documents, the assistant was sorry to say, the appointment couldn't be scheduled.

At that particular moment, we were on the road about an hour away from home, but I promised that she would have the material before the end of the day. With little time to spare, we rushed home. I filled out the paperwork she sent and faxed it back in time to meet the deadline.

Once the appointment was confirmed, I had a chance to relax and thought how important it had been for us to act, without delay, upon the inspiration I had received to make the calls. Otherwise, an appointment wouldn't have been possible so soon. I believe that God intervened and afforded us this unique opportunity, which represented a glimmer of hope to get us through our period of despair.

Friday arrived quickly. The time had come to meet the doctor who had unselfishly given of his limited time in order to help two lost souls who were strangers to him. He doesn't know the impact his actions had upon our lives, but I prayed that God would return the favor, should he ever need one!

When we reached the Enfield office, we noticed the whole complex was closed for the holiday weekend. As we drove in, the parking lot was also empty, so we waited in our car for evidence the doctor had arrived.

Within a few minutes, we saw someone standing inside the vestibule at the front of the office building. As we approached, a man opened the door and introduced himself as the doctor we were scheduled to meet. After he locked the door behind us, we followed him into the elevator. During the short ride in-between floors, we graciously thanked him for his kindness in affording us a portion of the little time he had available prior to his European trip.

Upon reaching the door to his office, he unlocked it. As we walked through the unlit office space, past the empty receptionist's desk, directly into his private office, the uniqueness of this remarkable opportunity was surreal.

The doctor turned on the lights to his office and asked us to be seated. While we settled in, he reviewed the medical reports I had faxed two days earlier, which included a diagnosis, blood work results, and a multitude of procedures my husband had undergone to date.

By now, the doctor was fully aware of my husband's condition, and although his voice was thoughtful and sympathetic, he wasted no time in pleasantries. In a straightforward manner, he wanted to know what my husband thought he could do for him since we all understood his case was terminal.

Although the doctor was blunt, we weren't offended by his frankness. We appreciated his candid approach. This had only made it easier to get past the sordid details of my husband's illness and right to the specific questions we had in mind.

My husband had made a mental list and wanted to know: 1) were there any experimental cancer treatments for pancreatic cancer, 2) might he possibly be a candidate for any ongoing studies, and 3) did the doctor know of any form of homeopathic remedy available to help with his swallowing disorder?

During this point in their conversation, I intervened. Although my husband and the doctor had discussed the mechanics of the difficulties he had been experiencing swallowing solids or liquids, I explained that my research had led us to believe his Parkinson's disease might be the cause.

Right away, the doctor recommended a feeding tube. My husband responded, although he was aware of this option, he was against it. He wouldn't consider this choice because he didn't want to spend his final days hooked up to tubes of any sort.

Since homeopathy was the only remaining medical treatment we thought might help treat his condition, my husband wanted to know if the doctor had any recommendations.

Unfortunately, the doctor replied, there was no magic pill available. My husband and I finally realized we had reached the end of the road, the place we so adamantly had been trying to avoid. Since surgery was no longer possible, and my husband's lack of nutritional intake had now become his biggest obstacle for a longer lifespan, we knew his prospects had finally run out.

We had hoped to find a resolution to his eating issue before he had to make the choice between chemotherapy or hospice care, but the illusive cure didn't seem to exist. In view of the fact that chemo appeared to be the only treatment option left, my husband needed guidance. Since the doctor was a disinterested third party and quite knowledgeable on the subject of cancer, my husband thought he might be able to offer a fresh outlook to the situation. Therefore, he asked the doctor's opinion about the merit of chemotherapy as a last resort.

"What would you do, if you were in my position?" was the million-dollar question my husband now asked.

When the doctor said that he considered my husband to be fortunate that he hadn't started chemotherapy, we were astonished. While reviewing the results from my husband's hospital stay, coupled with his significant loss of blood, the doctor suspected that indicators in his bloodwork results would play an important role in the choice my husband now faced.

"It takes time for the body to recuperate from large amounts of blood loss, before chemotherapy can become an option, and I have medical evidence which backs up my opinion," was the doctor's informed response. The doctor actually believed my husband might not have survived the first chemo treatment.

Since time was not an asset my husband had an abundance of, this revelation was an eye opener. The doctor's assessment of my husband's medical situation led him to believe that the cancer treatment which was intended to improve my husband's chances for survival, could be harmful instead.

Therefore, in response to my husband's question, the doctor believed the benefits chemotherapy could offer didn't outweigh the risks. He also agreed with my husband's position regarding a feeding tube. The doctor cautioned, "Pancreatic cancer is a very aggressive disease, and as time goes on it also becomes very painful. So, if I were in your position, I wouldn't choose a feeding tube either."

For some reason, once we had assessed all of the new information the doctor had supplied, we weren't devastated by his candor. His input into our life and death struggle had actually provided an unexpected calming effect.

From that point forward, we discussed the new experimental therapies which were on the horizon abroad. The doctor talked about encouraging research currently underway, which involved injecting living viruses into cancer patients in order to attack and kill cancer cells. In his opinion, this therapy would be the new cancer treatment in years to come. Unfortunately, the doctor didn't believe my husband would be around to benefit from this promising new research, because currently, it was still in its experimental stages.

Naturally, we asked if my husband could volunteer as a candidate for any of these studies. The doctor promised to look into this possibility but forewarned us, he most likely wouldn't be considered because he was over sixty-five and had Parkinson's disease.

While we began to wrap up our discussions, the doctor offered one final encouraging suggestion. It involved the use of medical marijuana. He proposed my husband try it because cannabis had been known to shrink tumors over time and might possibly help with my husband's Parkinson tremors. Though the doctor was uncertain if marijuana could offer any form of relief for my husband's eating disorder, he figured it might be worth a try. While this was a path we wouldn't have considered before, we now began to entertain the thought of researching marijuana as a possible alternative medication.

Considering the doctor's immediate travel plans, we couldn't thank him enough for the precious time he spent with us. Our appointment provided a wealth of beneficial information we were unaware of.

Due to the unusual circumstances in which we were afforded a golden opportunity to meet this doctor, we learned my husband's chances to live longer without treatment was most likely greater and less intrusive than his alternative choice of chemotherapy.

We believed we had received spiritual inspiration through God's graces, which led us to this unique opportunity. The information we received, which weighed heavily in the balance of my husband's final decision, aided him in his search for a path to follow.

It is important to remember, although a solution may not provide a cure, the resolution of difficult decisions we have to make along life's journey can be extremely comforting.

CHAPTER 21

His Fight to Live

Following our appointment with the naturopathic doctor, a calmness seemed to take over my husband's temperament. He was no longer anxious and seemed rather mellow, even though his future was uncertain. Now that we had crossed the last barrier and it appeared his options had expired, he seemed to have put the matter behind him, because he began to act as though life was back to normal and nothing was wrong.

Although the time had come to make his final choice between chemotherapy and hospice care, neither one of us was anxious to take this final step. Following the naturopathic doctor's appointment, I asked if he wanted me to schedule an appointment with the oncology department at the VA. When he declined my offer, I wasn't going to ask again. After all, I didn't want to walk down that road either, for I was content with the status quo as well.

Procrastination wasn't in our nature. Only now, a shared silence on this subject existed between us. The old saying, out of sight, out of mind, described in a nutshell how we chose to cope with the situation, at least for a while.

About a week passed before we received a call from the Providence VA to schedule an appointment. Our mutual effort to avoid this topic ended with this call, and the time to address his painful decision suddenly rose to the surface. In response to the request, I asked the caller to wait, so I could speak with my husband to see if he wanted to schedule an appointment at this time.

His annoyed response was, "No!"

I totally understood how he felt, and said, "I will pass on the message."

When I picked up the phone, I told the woman, "He isn't ready yet. We will be in touch when he is."

She compassionately replied, "I understand. Tell your husband to take his time. When he is ready, we will be there for him." My husband and I both understood that sooner or later he would have to choose between his fight to live . . . or decide on his journey to die . . . but for the moment, we needed a break from the entire emotionally painful ordeal.

The next week passed peacefully and life went on as though nothing was wrong. My husband had no other medical appointments scheduled, so on the surface, it felt as though he wasn't sick. Approximately two weeks after we had met with the naturopathic doctor, my husband finally asked me to call the VA to arrange a meeting. Once the appointment was scheduled, we didn't discuss his decision ahead of time, and I didn't bring the subject up, because I was afraid to hear his answer.

On the one hand, I wasn't certain if he had already decided his fate. On the other hand, I wondered if he was tormented by the difficult choice he needed to make. Although we both understood chemotherapy was extremely risky, when your life was on the line, it wasn't easy to walk away from the only option available.

When the appointment date arrived, during our long drive to the Providence VA, we avoided discussing the final decision he needed to make. Although our conversation wasn't cheerful by any means, we still managed to maintain a pleasant dialog between us, sharing pleasant memories, which had become our daily dose of sunshine while the ominous clouds of heart-ache loomed around us.

One would think that the drive would have been long and tedious, but the time passed quickly while we supportively interacted in as enjoyable a conversation as possible, under the circumstances. Before we knew it, we had arrived at the hospital.

In the reception area where we sat, it felt like only minutes had passed before my husband's name was called. I silently wished that we could have had hours longer to wait before we were led to the area where he would determine his fate.

Now that we were in the examination room, I sat fidgeting in my seat while I thought, "Dear Lord, is this a bad dream from which I will awaken? Or, if it is Your will, please guide him down the proper path!"

My thoughts were interrupted when a young intern entered the room to cover the preliminary updates of my husband's condition. We hadn't met him before, and I could tell my emotional sniffles made him feel a little bit uncomfortable.

Once he completed his short report, he asked, "Do you have any questions before I leave?"

My husband replied, "We are all set."

As he left the room, the intern looked relieved and anxious to escape the sadness of our situation, for he was well aware of the reason we were there.

It seemed like only a minute or two had passed before the head oncology doctor and two other women entered the small room. She reviewed my husband's latest biopsy results before she began to discuss the mortality statistics associated with his disease, which, of course, we had already heard many times before.

When she asked how my husband was feeling, he said his worsening swallowing disorder was his main concern.

Updated with new information from the naturopathic doctor's appointment, my husband now had reservations about the negative effects chemotherapy might have on his life expectancy. He wanted the oncology doctor's interpretation of the naturopathic doctor's misgivings regarding chemotherapy treatment.

The doctor didn't agree or disagree with the facts my husband presented. She just reaffirmed what she had told us at our last appointment, "Chemotherapy will neither cure nor extend your life for any substantial amount of time, if at all."

Although I could no longer control the tears which slowly rolled down my cheeks, my husband was totally composed. He showed no emotion as his final options were being weighed.

In an effort to help him decide, the doctor discussed the reason most pancreatic cancer patients refuse further treatment. With kindness in her voice, she explained, "Treatment will require you to spend the rest of your life in and out of hospitals without any hope of a cure."

Since we had no idea what to expect, one of the social service women picked up where the doctor left off. She began to discuss how the transfer of medical services from the VA to Hospice Care would take effect. She made it clear, "Should you decide to accept Hospice Care, all medical treatment available to fight your cancer stops; and only comfort care is administered through Hospice Care from that day forward. Once the transition takes effect, all emergency services will be provided through Hospice. Except for your medication needs, which will continue to be processed through the VA system, VA medical services will no longer be available to you."

In the doctor's final closing argument, she repeated the remarks we heard at our last meeting, "If you choose Hospice Care, you will be treated at home and allowed to die with dignity."

After a moment of silence, my husband declined further VA treatment and opted for Hospice services instead. He was unemotional, but had a look of determination on his face when he declared his decision.

Overcome with grief upon hearing our battle was lost, I cried uncontrollably. The doctor put her arm around my shoulder to comfort me. I struggled to gain control of my emotions in order to portray the strong woman my husband expected me to be.

The change in care would take place immediately. The doctor left the room after one of the assistants informed us that she would schedule an appointment for a Hospice nurse to visit our home the following day.

It wasn't as though my husband was a baby, who would be thrown out with the bath water. We were told, should he desire, his VA medical services could be reinstated at any time. It was made clear, however, in order to do so, he would have to contact the VA, request reinstatement of his medical benefits and withdraw from the Hospice Care benefits, since both services couldn't be accessed at the same time.

Up until now, I hadn't realized Hospice Care only serviced terminally ill patients. How naive I was. Of course, I knew my husband was dying, but the transfer of his medical services made his death feel so imminent.

I was emotionally drained because I didn't expect the reassignment to happen so quickly. I guess, I really didn't know what to expect.

Now that my husband's decision had been made, I was overcome with sorrow. As we sat alone in the room, the quiet was deafening. Currently, neither one of us was able to speak about his upcoming Hospice appointment . . . his prelude to death.

It didn't take long before one of the social services women returned. She provided me with the name and phone number of the Hospice Care unit my husband was assigned to and advised us that we had an appointment scheduled for the following day at our home to officially register my husband into the Hospice Care program.

In just minutes, it was over and done with, and my husband was no longer a VA patient. As soon as the transfer was finalized, I suddenly felt empty. It was as though a beautiful friendship had ended. The VA Medical Center was the place where my husband always felt comfortable and secure in his treatment throughout the years. Every time I called for information or to schedule an appointment, I had always been greeted by caring staff members who did their best to provide excellent services, which we undoubtedly appreciated considering the volume of patients they routinely handled.

Although my husband didn't particularly enjoy going to the doctor, we both knew he would miss his primary care doctor, with his cheery smile and dedicated values, who had worked so hard to keep him healthy. Now, suddenly, we were headed into uncharted territory.

After we left the examination room for the last time and walked down the familiar corridors we had traveled so many times together, my husband hopelessly said, "I will never walk down these halls again."

We both felt saddened as this chapter in our lives had come to an end, and the truth of our situation became factual.

Consequently, on July 22nd, the one piece of hope I had held onto for so long, that we would find an answer to keep my husband alive, died within me . . . as we took our final walk to the car and then drove away.

CHAPTER 22

He Just Wanted to Be Left Alone

We had spent the first three weeks of the month trying to live a resemblance of a normal life until the 22nd of July, when my husband took the plunge. He left behind his losing battle against pancreatic cancer, when he agreed to register for Hospice Care in order to salvage some tiny bit of enjoyment life may still have to offer during the final portion of his journey.

It was hard to believe in about a week August would already begin. The fact that the clock was quickly ticking away was constantly on my mind, but I refused to allow this thought to interfere with our attempt to enjoy the remainder of our time together.

Since my husband had transferred his medical treatment from the VA to Hospice Care, he was about to embark upon a brand-new territory of health care services, and I could tell by his lack of enthusiasm that he wasn't looking forward to it. There was no question in my mind, a structured medical service wasn't high on his list of priorities because it represented a constant reminder of his declining health . . . and besides, he didn't like change.

After spending almost fifty years of our lives together, I knew my husband well. At this point, after all he had been through, he just wanted to be left alone; but neither of us were naive enough to believe we could travel his final journey alone, without at least some form of a safety net. Therefore, Hospice Care became the security blanket we would depend upon when the going got rough.

Since I would be the survivor and primary caregiver in our relationship, I privately worried if I was up to the challenge. Would I be able to handle his needs during the majority of the days and especially the nights once his illness required round-the-clock care?

I never shared my fears with my husband. I didn't want to overburden him. I couldn't imagine how he handled his own mortality without unloading his anxiety upon me. It took a special type of person to play the hand he was dealt.

So, I guess you could say, by working together, my husband and I made the best of a lousy situation. When he decided to select Hospice Care, we both benefited. It enabled me to try to grant his wish to remain at home until he died, because now I had access to experienced medical services to assist me as we both tried to brave the inevitable tragedy which lay ahead.

Most importantly, I put my faith in God. I prayed The Lord would provide the strength we needed to make it through this difficult ordeal together, and grant me the wisdom to understand what I needed to do to make my husband's final journey peaceful.

Now, the time had come to blend the new health services into our fragile world. In anticipation of the arrival of the Hospice Care Service nurse, I settled into my comfortable office chair to do paperwork, while my husband sat on the front porch soaking up the early morning sun. Because I hated waiting anxiously for things to happen, I found it easier to engross myself in work, instead of watching the clock for our appointment time to slowly arrive.

As the time drew near for the nurse's arrival, the phone rang. A woman's voice responded when I said "Hello."

She identified herself as the Hospice nurse and said she was running about an hour late. She asked, "Will that be okay?" If not, she would have to reschedule for some time later that afternoon.

Feeling as though we were starting off on the wrong foot, I was a little annoyed, but I couldn't disregard the fact that she had at least bothered to call. After all, in this day and age, courtesy was no longer considered to be the norm, and I appreciated her effort to let us know she would be late.

Actually, the time delay really didn't matter because we didn't have any place to go. So, I replied, "It will be fine."

The call ended quickly, and it didn't take long for me to get wrapped up in my paperwork again. Suddenly, my concentration was broken when I heard a car traveling down our driveway. Since I had been occupied paying bills and balancing my checkbook, I hadn't realized how quickly the hour had passed.

When I walked over and opened the side door to see who it was, a smiling face emerged from behind the wheel of the car. With her arms full, balancing a bag full of paperwork and her computer, I invited her in and tried to lighten her load by grabbing her papers and putting them on the desk. Once inside and settled down, she shook my hand. She introduced herself as the Hospice nurse and again apologized, explaining how a mix up in her scheduling had been the cause for her delay.

Immediately, I was impressed with her friendly mannerism, and as I offered her a seat, my husband entered the room. Since he was not enthusiastic on the whole idea, I hoped the appointment would go smoothly. Only time would tell how everyone would respond to this new state of affairs.

The nurse was a very pleasant woman, with a bubbly personality. Right away, my husband gave her a hard time, in his fun-loving way. He was a kidder. If you could take his ribbing, you were in.

You could tell she was a trooper, for she responded in kind, and they hit it off right from the start. In short order, she appeared to feel right at home. By the time she left, it felt like we had been friends forever.

When I questioned if she would be my husband's permanent nurse, she insinuated that it hadn't been decided as of yet.

Her statement led me to assume her assignment would depend upon whether or not she wanted to travel the distance because she had mentioned it was a long drive from her house to ours.

Due to the fact we weren't familiar with Hospice Care, she explained the main purpose for today's appointment was to register my husband for Hospice services. My husband needed to sign some forms in order to accept their agency as his Hospice provider. He also needed to confirm the accuracy of his medical diagnosis, which had already been provided to this Hospice Agency by the VA representative who initially scheduled the appointment.

She discussed the services we could expect through Hospice Care and provided additional paperwork to explain the services in detail. After the introductory portion of our appointment was over, we learned Hospice services didn't support around-the-clock, in-home nursing care, although in the event of emergencies, someone was available for limited services 24-hours a day.

We were both satisfied with the terms of the agreement. Neither my husband nor I wanted an intrusion into our life until it was absolutely necessary, so the fact that the services were limited was perfectly acceptable. We were loners, who enjoyed the quiet solitude our earlier retirement had previously afforded us, and we hoped the Hospice services wouldn't interfere with our desire to maintain our privacy.

During our initial appointment, aside from his Parkinson symptoms, my husband's robust and outward physical appearance defied the disease that raged within. When the nurse first met my husband, she remarked, "If you hadn't told me you were the patient, I wouldn't have known you were sick. You don't look drawn or weak like most of my cancer patients do."

Even though he had lost weight, my husband still had a ruggedness to his build from all his years of hard, physical labor, and his olive complexion hadn't taken on the dull-grayish color associated with a terminal illness. I assumed my husband's body currently subsisted off his muscular frame, but worried how long he could survive since his nutritional intake was no longer sufficient to sustain his existence for an extended period of time.

We were hopeful her positive observation might indicate he still had time on his side.

Our conversation eventually turned to the subject of medical marijuana. My husband brought up the naturopathic doctor we recently met, who suggested marijuana might help with his pain or possibly control his tremors, which were symptomatic of his Parkinson's disease. In order to take advantage of her medical expertise, he asked her opinion on the matter.

Since it was obvious from his question that my husband was not a recreational user of illegal drugs, she explained, "Some people might get relief. On the other hand, those people who have never used drugs, might find the side effects objectionable."

She expanded her initial comments by noting, even though marijuana provided some form of relief for pain and tremors, many people who weren't accustomed to this type of drug might not enjoy the loss of mind control which accompanied its use.

Despite this fact, she agreed with the argument that marijuana might be beneficial. She added, "The choice is a personal one only you can make."

Once the drug issue was satisfactorily examined, our conversation turned to the subject of the nursing, in-home visit, frequency requirements. Because my husband wasn't interested in receiving weekly checkups, he insisted his appointments be limited to bi-monthly meetings.

In his mind's eye, he didn't like receiving medical care. He couldn't legitimize a reason to take his blood pressure or update his health records on a weekly basis. From his point of view, just because he was dying, it didn't mandate his compliance to a structured appointment schedule.

He felt he was still in charge and wanted to decide if and when medical services would be rendered. Besides, it was his understanding that Hospice Care was supposed to assist you, when you needed it!

Of course, when the situation warranted, he agreed to be flexible. But for the time being, he didn't want a constant reminder he was dying. He told the nurse, his main reason for registering at this time was to cover his at-home medical or emergency services and unforeseen medical equipment requirements.

Having dealt with so many terminally ill patients throughout her career, the nurse concurred with his rationalization. She respected him, as well as his desire to remain independent for as long as he could, and she readily agreed with his request. Therefore, she scheduled his appointments at two-week intervals.

While on her way out the door, with a smile and a wink, she said he could call the office anytime if he needed help. She wanted him to know that the Hospice Care helpline was available 24-hours a day.

This comforting thought helped ease my concerns.

When she called the next day, we were happy to learn that she would be his nurse and liaison, because she had been assigned to his case. She was a good fit at this challenging time in our lives.

CHAPTER 23

Experiencing Life to Its Fullest

Once the Hospice nurse left, I followed my husband to his favorite spot, the outside front porch, where he quickly settled down into his chair. After I knew he was comfortable, I went to the side gate to let the dogs out, so they could lay down and relax near us while we enjoyed the peace and quiet of the outdoors. My husband turned on the small radio he kept outside to an oldies channel, and only the occasional sounds of birds chirping could be heard over the low volume of the rock and roll music we began to enjoy.

While we sat and relished each other's company, in the stillness of our cozy, remote refuge, with all the trees in full bloom, it brought back recollections of the lazy days of summer when we were dating and had nothing to do . . . but enjoy doing nothing together. Those were some of my favorite memories.

My husband broke our tranquil silence when he asked me what I thought about contacting the State of CT to obtain information about the Medical Marijuana Program. Since his diagnosis, he hadn't suggested we look into any alternative treatment other than the VA options he pursued. All along, I had been the one who actively investigated every opportunity I could think of in order to search out effective treatments for his illness.

His request was music to my ears. I would be thrilled to find out more information, in the hopes he would find some benefit through its use. We discussed the next step we would need to take and agreed, the best approach would be to call one of the locally authorized medical marijuana clinics to find out how the process worked.

There was a clinic located about twenty minutes from where we lived, and I figured now was as good a time as any to place a call. The local representative I reached explained there were various forms of marijuana to choose from, which could be either smoked or eaten. She advised me that the effects varied and were subject to the supplier's specific intended useful purpose. Depending upon the relief a patient sought, the benefits of the various products would be explained at the time of purchase, once the patient was registered with the State of CT Marijuana Program and was in a position to buy the product.

In response to the questions I asked about the types of maladies marijuana is supposed to help, she suggested we contact one of the area doctors who could register my husband into the program. The woman felt a doctor would be more qualified to discuss the advantages and disadvantages associated with the use of marijuana, depending upon the illness. In case my husband was interested, she provided me with a short list of names and phone numbers of the local doctors involved in the program.

After a few minutes of informative conversation, I thought her advice made sense. So as soon as our discussion ended, I rejoined my husband on the porch in order to bring him up to date. Once we discussed the details, he agreed with her recommendations and suggested that I schedule an appointment.

Due to the fact that long drives were becoming tiresome for my husband, we decided to contact the closest doctor, who was located in Guilford, CT. I called and left a message on Thursday, detailing my husband's situation, and requested a return call to arrange a meeting. The doctor called back the next day and scheduled an appointment for the 28th of July, which was Tuesday of the following week.

His office, located in the southern part of Guilford Center, is situated in a quaint little portion of Guilford's shoreline community, which offers appealing shops and intimate little restaurants. Had my husband not been sick, the warm atmosphere of this scenic municipality would have been an enjoyable destination spot to shop and grab a bite to eat.

Since we hadn't been to this part of Guilford before, when we arrived in town the GPS seemed to have gotten confused, so I stopped and walked into one of the local shops to get directions.

As it turned out, the doctor's office was located directly across the street from where we were currently parked. Had we turned left, instead of following the turn right command our GPS had specified, we would have been there already.

It was an easy fix. Within a few minutes, we maneuvered our way across the busy intersection, parked the car and located the appropriate building where the doctor's office was located.

Apparently the doctor shared a building complex and receptionist with other professionals, which seemed to be a common practice in this day and age. Upon reaching the receptionist's desk, we were instructed to go to the second floor, which was where the doctor's suite was located. Since his office door was locked, we sat in the waiting area outside of his office. When he arrived shortly thereafter, we were escorted into his private office and offered a seat.

The room we entered was small, but cozy. It contained large, maroon leather chairs, and a bookcase-lined wall filled with medical journal, located behind an attractive cherry wooden desk. All things considered, I was most impressed with the pretty view of the picturesque street below.

Now that we were nestled in the soft cushiony chairs in front of the doctor's desk, in order to break the ice, we chatted for a few moments. During this introductory portion of our meeting, my husband mentioned how life had turned out for him after his military service in Vietnam, and he also explained the service connection between his Parkinson's disease and Agent Orange exposure.

During their conversation, the doctor noted that he was retired military. He happened to have served as a physician in Vietnam during the same period of time my husband had served, in the 60's. This disclosure made me feel as though an unspoken bond had quickly developed. I suddenly got the impression that the friendly conversation was now between one Vietnam Vet to another, instead of between doctor and patient. It was obvious to me that the distinction of rank was no longer relevant as it would have been had they both been back in Vietnam so many years ago.

After discussing our construction and development business and how he had established himself as a businessman in our community, I could tell my husband felt comfortable and on a level playing field with the doctor. I gathered, from the relaxed atmosphere and the doctor's friendly responses, the feeling appeared to be mutual.

During the conversation, we learned the doctor handled a limited clientele since his military retirement, and this was the reason we weren't being rushed through our appointment.

Once the two of them finished reminiscing, we got down to business and the conversation finally turned to the reason for the meeting. The time had come to give the doctor a copy of the hospice status sheet, which confirmed my husband's terminal diagnosis and qualified him for admittance into our state's Marijuana Program.

After he completed his review of the medical documents, the doctor asked my husband what symptoms he hoped to improve through the use of marijuana?

As usual, the most sought-after relief related to my husband's swallowing issues, because now he was choking when he tried to eat or drink. My husband believed as this condition worsened, his life expectancy diminished along with these capabilities. Of course, pain was a constant part of his life, but in addition to the eating disorder, his Parkinson's induced tremors were an annoyance as well.

130

We were surprised to learn that the doctor was very familiar with Parkinson's. A family member of his suffered from the disease as well. Unfortunately, he didn't believe marijuana would help the Parkinson's induced swallowing issue, but he thought my husband might benefit from pain relief, as well as a possible reduction to his tremors.

Cautiously, the doctor alluded to the fact that marijuana may help kill cancer cells over a period of time, but he wasn't hopeful it would be beneficial in fighting pancreatic cancer. Nevertheless, he believed different forms of marijuana buds would help my husband achieve a better night's sleep and relief from his pain.

The doctor discussed the drug's negative side effects as well. Since these concerns varied from person to person, he backed up what the hospice nurse had previously said. Only my husband could determine if the positive results outweighed the negative ones.

Because marijuana offered pain relief, I suggested my husband try it and learn, for himself, whether it helped him in any positive way. If by some miracle it improved his swallowing issues, that would be an added benefit, but we weren't optimistic of this result. Ultimately, I told my husband if he didn't like the side effects, he could stop at any time. All things considered, the doctor suggested my husband had nothing to lose by enrolling, especially since his cancer was terminal.

Clearly, this rational made sense, so my husband agreed. The doctor then registered him on the state's Medical Marijuana website while we were still in his office. Now that the doctor's portion of the state's form was completed, he said it would take a few days before I could access my husband's portion of the application, which involved filling out the State of CT patient form, submitting a passport picture and paying a fee.

As we were leaving the doctor's office, he said we could call him if we ran into any trouble completing the paperwork.

Two days later, I filled out the online patient form, and we waited for his card to arrive in the mail. Not wanting to seem anxious, after a few weeks had passed and no card had been issued, I called the state agency to inquire how his request had progressed. I was surprised to learn his application hadn't even been looked at and was told, the program had so many submissions in process, it usually took a few months for an approval to be issued.

When I explained that my husband was under hospice care and dying, the State worker I spoke with became very compassionate. She instructed me to fax evidence of his hospice care, and his ID card arrived in the mail shortly thereafter. He was now qualified to make purchases at any local CT approved marijuana dispensary.

To make a long story short, he tried a few different variations of the drugs and was not impressed. Since he was already challenged by unsteadiness, loss of equilibrium, freezing in place, etc., which were side effects of his Parkinson's disease; the confusion, mind fog, loss of ability to think rationally and additional exhaustion, which he associated with the drug use, were unacceptable to him.

Although he gave it a try, my husband decided the drugs were not to his liking, so he terminated their use. He wanted to preserve his ability to think and communicate with me for as long as he could. While the marijuana had helped with his pain, he chose clarity of mind over his physical discomfort in this matter.

It truly amazed me how intent he was upon experiencing life to its fullest, even though he knew the end was near.

CHAPTER 24

The Difficult Task

The month of July had now passed, another page on the calendar had turned, and August was upon us. I was thankful my husband had been enjoying the warm weather during his favorite time of year, especially since our rides to nowhere had started to become too tiring.

A good portion of his time was now spent at home. Although he appeared to be relaxed, I soon realized he now spent his time planning what he could do to help make things easier for me before he died.

Since my husband knew our present home would be too much for me to maintain on my own, he wanted to know where I intended to live once I sold our home. He was well aware how difficult this transition would be, and he was surprised to learn that I had no plans. I hadn't thought that far ahead. At the moment, my only concern was that he would die in the house we had shared as our home for so many happy years.

He could tell I was sad when I said, "I will figure it out when the time comes."

My revelation concerned him. So, he suggested, if I wanted, we could drive around and look at existing homes and neighborhoods. We could check to see what properties were available . . . which we did.

Neither of us were happy with the existing choices, because the homes were either too old, 2-story or too much money. When we were still in the construction business, we specialized in one-story, single-family retirement homes. My husband suggested that we had the ideal house plan to tweak if I was willing to build it on my own. Since we already owned an extra building lot in our current neighborhood, he recommended I build a smaller home in an area I was familiar with.

The land already had a special meaning to me because we often walked it together during our walkabouts, but I worried about my ability to build a new house and deal with his death at the same time. My husband reassured me by saying, "You have been in the business for almost as long as I have and are more than capable to handle the job on your own."

Building a new house on this land was my first choice, and his encouragement did the trick. While he was still capable, he even viewed the on-site plot plan layout with the engineer. He had a gift when it came to visualizing the finished product. He expertly set the clearing parameter, and even made certain the house would be properly situated on the lot, as he had always envisioned it.

My decision brought him relief because now he knew I had a plan. Selling our house and building a new one would be a difficult task for me to complete, but looking back, it was definitely the right choice. I have been forever grateful for my husband's guidance during this traumatic time in my life.

Once this decision was behind us, my husband caught me off guard when he proclaimed, "It's time we go to the funeral home to make our funeral arrangements while I am still able to leave the house."

Remarkably, he was calm and spoke as though he suggested we go to the grocery store to buy some milk. On the other hand, I was shocked and speechless when the reality of what he requested sank in.

As of yet, I hadn't accepted the fact he would die in the foreseeable future. No matter how ominously the dark storm clouds swirled around us, I couldn't think about his death or how I would handle it.

On the other hand, he wanted to make sure my funeral would be taken care of as well as his, so he wanted them planned together. This way our choices would be made together, as though we had planned our funerals before his illness necessitated our current action.

At the time he first suggested the idea, I was against it. Once I had a chance to get over the initial shock, I realized he was right. It just wasn't going to be easy.

I sensed compassion in his effort to spare me the pain of facing the inevitable alone. His thoughtfulness made the execution of the process a lot easier to deal with because he took control over this difficult mission.

Obviously, it would have been much easier if we had completed our funeral arrangements when we were both healthy. Unfortunately, it wasn't a high priority on our bucket list. So now, we needed to act, or I would be making my husband's funeral arrangements on my own.

Moving ahead, we needed to decide where we should go to get information and a price. The funeral home our families had used in the past had been sold to a conglomerate a few years back. Although it was still being managed by the same funeral director who was an old friend of my husband, I asked if we could go elsewhere. I thought it would be easier for me to discuss his approaching funeral with a stranger than with someone we knew, and my husband agreed.

During times like this, decisions are difficult to make. Often you have to go with your gut and live with the consequences, hoping you haven't caused hard feelings along the way. So, I called another funeral home and scheduled an appointment for the next morning. The mere fact that I had placed the call took its toll on me. For the rest of the day, I fought an internal emotional battle to remain positive, to perpetuate the good intention my husband had so unselfishly put into motion.

Neither one of us had an appetite when morning arrived, so we skipped the tiny breakfast we normally would have eaten and headed out to tackle our quest. We remained quiet during our short drive to the funeral home and avoided discussing the reason for our trip.

As soon as we arrived, I took a deep breath, opened the car door and stepped out. When I walked over and reached my husband's side, I grabbed his arm for moral support. As we climbed the stairs, before we had a chance to ring the bell, the funeral home representative had already opened the door. Once we entered the building, the woman led us down a hallway to a large, windowless room where two seats were set out in front of a lonely desk. She pointed toward the chairs and asked us to be seated. We were both given duplicate funeral information packets which included a basic price list, plus multiple upgrade options, for our review.

At the start of our appointment, we hadn't mentioned the fact that my husband was dying. As far as the representative was concerned, there was no imminent need for their services. But I knew the truth, and this knowledge was tearing me apart. I had hoped to be able to survive the appointment without breaking down, but I was suddenly overcome with sadness and struggled to keep my composure. After all, we weren't there to order pre-arranged funeral contracts; this was for real!

After finishing the description of the basic package, the representative continued to discuss the extra options which were available at an additional cost. By now, I had a difficult time keeping everything straight in my mind.

My stress level, most certainly, must have compounded my frustration, because by the time she finished her presentation, I wasn't ready to make any decisions. When the appointment ended, we gathered the paperwork, thanked the woman for her help, and left. I was relieved that I hadn't been in a sudden-death scenario which would have required immediate action. The whole situation was overwhelming.

Because I had no interest in discussing the matter any further, the moment we got home, I put the papers on the table and left the packet untouched.

The next morning, my husband picked up the pamphlets and looked over all of the figures. After reading them through, he told me he thought the prices were high. Now, he wanted me to contact another funeral home, to comparison shop. Unlike me, he wasn't saddened by our appointment. Actually, he had developed an inquisitiveness, which seemed to have sparked his interest. Before making a decision, he wanted to know if all funeral homes charged the same price.

At first, I couldn't bear the thought of going through the process all over again, but he won me over once I took the time to review the figures as well. Now, I also became curious and wondered, did the services and prices vary from one establishment to another?

When a loved one dies unexpectedly, there is little time available to make decisions and complete final arrangements. You are in the midst of grief and unable to think. You tend to make decisions with your heart and not your head. Once I had time to think, I accepted my husband's logical approach to this expensive endeavor. His comparison pricing suggestion became a challenge, and his positive attitude made it easier for me to comply with his subsequent request.

In search of an alternative, I reviewed other local funeral homes on the internet. One establishment, a husband and wife partnership, stood out from all the rest. The concept of a family-run business appealed to us both. We decided that I would call and schedule a consultation.

This time, when we arrived for our appointment and rang the bell, it was the funeral director who answered the door. He introduced himself as the owner and then led us into his office.

It was a cozy room, with curtains on the windows. There was a small, round table with four chairs, where he invited us to sit. As we began to talk, I immediately felt at ease. We told the proprietor that we wanted prices for pre-paid funerals, but didn't let on we had already priced a package at a competitor's establishment.

After muddling through the confusing funeral costs from the previous appointment and totaling the options we felt would be most suitable for the funerals we had in mind, my husband and I were much better prepared for this meeting.

The owner was personable and easygoing. Instead of jumping right into the details of funeral arrangements and their cost, he explained how the funeral home had been opened many years ago by his father. Only now, he and his wife ran the business since his father was getting on in years. We carried on a very pleasant conversation about everything under the sun, except funerals. There was no pressure on his part to get down to business. Soon, it felt like we were old friends.

Eventually we disclosed the real purpose for our meeting, and the owner was shocked to learn my husband's funeral would take place within the year. Since my husband's illness wasn't obvious, the funeral director didn't expect to hear that my husband was dying and only had a few months left to live. By now, he had taken a liking to us both, and I could tell by his expression, he was truly saddened by the news.

In order to fill in the blanks for his early passing, my husband divulged his Parkinson's disease and Agent Orange complications. As we continued our conversation, we developed a friendlier relationship and learned that the owner's father suffered from Parkinson's as well. Our sharing of a common thread of this debilitating illness seemed to tighten the newly created bond between us.

It wasn't the fact that his prices were more reasonable; the proprietor's friendly attitude had transformed an extremely distressing situation into a peaceful one, due to his ability to make strangers feel at home.

There was no need to search any further. We knew we had come to terms with the difficult task that lay ahead. In accordance with my husband's wishes, both of our funeral arrangements had now been decided.

By mid-August, the weather was still warm and the market for convertibles was still good, so my husband wanted to discuss his plan to sell his new sports car. Because I didn't want him to go through the sadness of selling his pride and joy, I told him I would take care of it when the time was right.

He knew I didn't intend to keep the car, and he understood its value would go down if I held onto it till spring. Furthermore, he cautioned, "You won't have anywhere to keep it if you sell the house right away. Besides, it will be one less thing for you to worry about."

Of course, I knew he was right. So, on the 31st of August, we sold the vehicle to a car dealership. This transaction was difficult. I could see the sadness in his eyes, when we drove away in the back seat of my brother-in-law's car while my husband's shiny maroon convertible disappeared from our view . . . for his car remained in front of the show room door where he had parked it.

At the same time, he wanted me to have a safe car for winter driving. So, my husband recommended I trade in my current vehicle for a four-wheel-drive SUV. In order to calm his concerns, within a week, we completed that transaction as well. Before he became completely housebound, this was the last official decision we made together as a couple.

He was finally at peace and satisfied. We had addressed the issues which worried him most, the ones he felt competent we could do something about while he was still able to. Sadly, from then on, all new decisions would be up to me.

CHAPTER 25

Spiritual Experiences

The time has come to expand on the spiritual side of my life, which in my youth, I would describe more as an innocent's perception of good vs. evil. In my early teens, my spiritual activities started with a friend's introduction to a Ouija board. Let me be the first to say, although it was marketed as a game, it was no toy.

It was the early 1960's, and my sister and I were spending time with a grade-school acquaintance at her parents' two-family home in Brooklyn, New York. Since Brooklyn's summers can be so hot that the tar would melt in the streets, the best place to be was in the shade, under a tree somewhere. Our friend's house had the perfect tree. So, we sat on the steps which led to her front door, trying to figure out what we could do that wouldn't be too exhausting because of the heat. Back in those days air conditioning wasn't a luxury our families could afford, and during the summertime, playing outside was the norm.

Suddenly, our friend had an idea. She got up and went into her house. A few minutes later, she emerged with a game in her arms, a Ouija board. When she walked down the stairs and sat down between my sister and me, she told us the purpose of the game was to foretell the future. When she took the board out of the box and placed it on her lap, her instructions were simple. Ask a question, and the board will give you the answer.

Though unfamiliar with the game, she made it sound like fun, so we agreed to give it a try.

In order to play, two people needed to partake in the activities. The participants placed their fingers, using both hands, on a wooden or plastic heart-shaped cast, which came to a point, known as a planchette. When an inquiry was made, the planchette glided along and then hesitated, pointing out selected letters, numbers, or yes and no answers on the board. When you combined the letters, words were formed, which in turn created phrases or sentences to answer your question.

My sister was the first to partner with our friend, and I was amazed to see the speed at which the planchette traveled across the board. It moved so fast, I couldn't keep up with its selections. Since our friend was already a wiz at playing the game, within seconds, she announced the answer to a question one of us had asked.

Once it was my turn to play, as hard as I tried, I couldn't get the planchette to budge. Disillusioned, I transferred control back to my sister and our friend. When I asked, "Why won't it work for me?" the response came quickly, "You don't believe."

At the moment, although I didn't understand what this statement meant, soon enough, I learned there was a more ominous side to this game for those who delve too deep.

Young and naive at this point in time, that particular remark made the answers seem even more fascinating. Now, I thought, it must truly be something mystical that predicted my future through the movement of the planchette.

Even though I was unable to actively participate, I was intrigued. Since I had just become a teenager that summer and wasn't dating as of yet, the hope of finding true love was on my mind. Most importantly, I wanted to know who I would marry and how many children we would have.

Instantaneously, our friend provided a young man's first name, followed by the announcement, I would have three children. I remember being disappointed when I thought, "I don't know anyone by that name."

I can't recall any of the other answers to questions we asked that day, but once we got tired of the game, I distinctly remember our friend describing scary scenarios she was dealing with in her bedroom. She talked about disturbing noises and scratching under her bed. She even mentioned guttural sounds and the feeling of something clawing at her bed sheets while she tried to sleep at night. She told us she was truly afraid.

Bearing in mind, she must have been troubled by these events, I asked her why she hadn't told her parents. She replied that she had, but they didn't believe her. Although at the time, I felt concerned for her well-being, I made no connection to her adept use of the Ouija board as a possible cause for these disturbing events.

Shortly thereafter, my family moved, and we lost contact with our friend. Once we settled into our new apartment and had time on our hands, I eventually asked my sister if she would share the cost of buying a Ouija board because I thought the game was entertaining and fun to play.

To make a long story short, we bought the game, and after persistent failed attempts, my sister and I watched in amazement when suddenly the planchette, without any manipulation on our part, effortlessly floated across the board as though on thin air, hovering over letters in answer to our requests. We were truly amazed.

For a while, all went well, and the game was fun; until one day, I inquisitively asked the board who was answering our questions. The response was so disturbing, I no longer desired to play the game.

Intuitively, we immediately discontinued the use of the board and planchette, thereby shutting down the messaging, and we never made contact again. Soon after, an evil feeling of uneasiness began to emanate from the closet, in the spare bedroom where the board was kept. I remember praying to God for protection and direction.

Thereafter, every time I entered the room where the game was stored, I was afraid, and soon I felt a strong inclination to throw the game away. Although my sister didn't encounter the same negativity that I sensed, she readily agreed. After I disposed of the Ouija board and it was no longer in the house, I continued to pray for God's protection, especially during the night. Soon the unpleasant feeling disappeared, the room's ambiance returned to normal, and I was no longer afraid. I believe we were fortunate to have avoided potentially dangerous consequences involving conceivable negative spiritual influences my sister and I were completely unprepared to handle.

In summary, the information we received while using the Ouija board seemed like harmless fun. Initially, it appeared as though we accessed a positive energy through our innocent use; until one day, a negative one emerged.

I mention this event to point out the fact that many people who seem to have a sensitivity to the spirit world have admitted to delving into a spirit board type of activity that I described. I have never written off the possibility that those experiences opened a veil for me between this world and the next.

It didn't take long for the memories of these events to fade from my mind. As time passed and I finally started to date, I never chose a boyfriend based upon the first name prediction I had been given through a board game so many years before. That would have been ridiculous.

Yet, when I first met my husband almost four years later, and we began to date, he didn't use his given first name and was known by a nickname instead. After dating for a while, our developing relationship led me to want to know more about him. When I finally got around to asking him his real name, that was the first time I realized it was the same name the Ouija board had predicted. Coincidentally, his letters from Vietnam spoke of his hopes to have three children when we were married. Were it not for my health, that part of the prediction might have come true as well.

Although the Ouija board may have predicted our paths would cross, like two ships in the night, our relationship had already blossomed, and it was by choice and not directive that we decided to combine our journeys and travel through life together.

I have always considered our meeting to be *the life-changing event* of my life. Although fate may have had a lot to do with our first encounter, I have no doubt, we were fortunate to have been able to realize the full potential spending our lives together afforded us. In our relationship, we imagined ourselves to be soulmates who were predestined to meet on Earth . . . who would spend eternity together once our journeys were complete.

Most of my life, I have been sensitive to a perception of the existence of supernatural activities in our world. I guess I could sum it up as a feeling that spirits lived amongst us, because I experienced eerie, unnerving feelings, which under certain circumstances made the hair on the back of my neck or arms rise without provocation. Despite a limited awareness that paranormal powers were present in our realm, and my Ouija board experiences, a major spiritual event did not occur in my life until early in our marriage, when I was in my late twenties.

Like most couples, there were always instances when my husband and I faced trials and tribulations. We always managed to get through them of our own accord, until one particular business crisis occurred which almost destroyed our fledgling construction business. When all of our attempts to rectify a contested subdivision situation failed, I went to bed and turned to God for His assistance. My profound impassioned plea, "Please God, help us, I don't know what else we can do," did not go unanswered.

That very night, I was awoken by a man's voice. It gave me instructions, which my husband suggested we follow, that immediately solved our stalemate.

Approximately 23 years would pass before another one of life's unexpected trials devastated me. All parents experience similar clashes, at one time or another, during the period of time their children grow into adulthood. It involved a difference of opinions, of viewpoints a mother and daughter may sometimes encounter, which caused discord in our existing harmony.

At that time, each night I went to bed with the same question, the same devout pray for intuition to understand the reasoning behind God's will, which was causing me such pain. Then, one night, the same male voice spoke to me again, and its answer took away the pain, which eventually led to resolution of the conflict. I will never forget the powerful message I received: *The event was not meant to hurt, it was meant to teach. Our children will never learn life's lessons unless they go out on their own, since we are all meant to live our own lives as we ourselves see fit.*

As a parent, this was a hard lesson to learn, and I found not only comfort but truth in God's message.

After this second spiritual inner voice experience, for some unknown reason, instead of my mind returning to its normal way of functioning, an explosion of otherworldly activities began to take place during the night, for which I had no explanation.

Shortly after receiving my insightful message, while asleep in bed one night, I suddenly awoke to a foggy, smoky cloud in our bedroom. The smoke obscured my vision of our TV, which sat on top of a bureau located on the opposite side of the room.

My heart pounded as I jumped out of bed and ran to the door to see if our house was on fire, but the hallway was clear. When I realized there was no smell to indicate any evidence of fire, I turned around to look back into the bedroom. The smoke had vanished, as though it had never existed. Rattled, but satisfied we were safe, I got back into bed and thought the event must have been a dream.

Soon, the smoke became a constant manifestation which interrupted my sleep, and I realized the materialization wasn't a dream. Eventually, the phenomena became so commonplace, I would remain in bed and watch in amazement as the smoke quickly dissolved before my eyes. When it vanished, although it wasn't instantaneous, it looked as though the fog had been sucked up by an invisible vacuum cleaner before it disappeared.

Eventually, I assumed the fog evaporated as a direct result of my initial fearful reaction to its presence. Then, after frequent encounters, I was no longer afraid and became curious instead. Once I accepted the existence of the anomaly, it lingered. During certain times, the smoke began to twirl, like a thunder storm of whirling winds. I was truly bewildered, yet fascinated by the different forms the manifestation managed to create. One time, the smoke actually split in half and flowed past me, traveling parallel to each side of my bed until it floated through the wall behind me, as though it had done so through the process of osmosis. Now, I began to wonder if the smoke had some form of intelligence because of its ability to do more than just appear and disappear.

Captivated by this mystery, I wanted to share my experience with someone other than my husband, who never personally experienced these events, but believed in their existence because of the many nights he would awaken to my frightened reaction. Whenever I stirred him from his sleep, as a result of my startled response, he always asked, "Is everything okay?" In time, since these experiences had become so commonplace, my standard reply would be, "It's only the smoke."

One day, while my sister and her husband were visiting, I brought up the subject of the fascinating smoky fog. When I mentioned my fears our house might have been on fire, my twin sister immediately perked up. She confessed that on more than one occasion, she had experienced similar thick smoke at her house. She even related an instance when she had fallen asleep on her couch and woke up to see her adjacent dining room filled with smoke. She described how she had gotten up to investigate, and when she was about to enter through the doorway, the fog immediately evaporated exactly as I portrayed it. As far as we were concerned, our similar experiences of this incredible phenomena was too much of a coincidence. My sister and I began to wonder, had our youthful Ouija board escapades opened our mind to a spiritual world beyond our own, which becomes more active during emotional events in our lives?

Although there is no way for us to prove these experiences occurred, one thing is certain, my sister and I have never felt threatened by these incidents, nor do we believe there is any evil associated with the activities. In fact, we are fascinated by this mystery, and hope, someday, to establish a logical reason for the manifestations.

While I am not a spiritual medium or expert on the subject of what happens to the soul after our death, I became captivated whenever I encountered these strange anomalies during the night. Although I am unable to explain the cause, I do believe these spiritual events are from the light and not the dark side of this fascinating domain.

It is my impression that a veil between our earthly realm and the world beyond our scope of knowledge has been penetrated. As I look back on these earlier events, I wonder if these activities were intended to be an introduction, or perhaps a preparation, for more intense spiritual encounters yet to come?

Over time, I have learned that it is the intensity of my anguish that perpetuates my experiences, because overcoming my sorrow causes the events to lessen, especially when my distress is under control.

My acceptance of the range of the spiritual activities, which continue to occur in my life, has allowed me to observe and accept the existence of a spiritual realm I believe is real.

CHAPTER 26

Seeing Orbs

For those of you who are not familiar with the paranormal phenomena known as orbs, I, myself, have been on the fence about the subject for a long while. I wasn't certain if they were spiritual energy, dust or tricks of photography. I have seen many photographs and television shows in which the manifestation of round circles of light, of various size and color, leaves one to wonder if they actually represent the evidence of spirits or are they a misinterpretation of natural events?

Most paranormal investigators aren't convinced that orbs associated with digital and film photography, infrared lights or reflective surfaces, which can cause orb-like appearances, are spirits. But, many in the paranormal community believe orbs that have their own light source, travel in unusual patterns, and are seen by the naked eye, are quite possibly paranormal in nature.

Up until now, orb interaction wasn't part of my spiritual resume. An incident, which occurred at the office of the funeral home director we chose to perform our services, is where I finally got off the fence.

As previously mentioned, our appointment with the funeral proprietor went well. When we neared the end of our meeting, after giving the go ahead to prepare the contracts, the owner left the room to bring back samples of the selections we would need to make. So, as not to dwell upon the funeral proceedings we were planning, while waiting for the owner to return, I slowly turned my head to take in all the details of the room. Contrary to what most people would think possible, out of the left corner of my eye, I spotted an anomaly. I was intrigued by a small, round milky-white object fluttering through the sunlight. It was located in a sunbeam, which was streaming through the window adjacent to my chair. There appeared to be an unusual amount of activity in a small section of the sunlight, at an elevation about a foot or two off the floor. At first I thought it was dust particles, whizzing through the air. Then, I noticed the unfamiliar object scurried from the sunlight, into the shadowy area under the table, in the vicinity of my feet.

On many occasions, I have witnessed the stormy rotation of dust particles in the sunlight, as the energy caused by the heat of the sun's rays helps create the movement of matter. I am not saying that dust particles are no longer able to move in the shade, since heat energy can still exist in such an environment, thus enabling movement to occur. What I am saying is that I find it difficult to see dust particles as they float through the air once they are no longer illuminated by the rays of the sun.

Therefore, I had no explanation for the object which emerged from the sunlight and continued to self-illuminate. I noted, with interest, that the entity was tiny, white and bursting with activity, fluttering like a tiny butterfly only much faster. I chuckled to myself, as I watched and became captivated by its actions, for it appeared to travel with a distinct purpose in mind.

Since I was currently in a funeral home, I thought the object might be an orb. In this particular instance, I believed the orb to be the spirit of a person who had recently died and, after leaving its body, didn't know where to go or what to do. It almost felt as though the object was trying to interact with me, in search of help, because it hovered around me like a new puppy craving the security of its littermates. But, then again, possibly the entity found itself in a brand-new spiritual environment and needed to investigate in order to find its way. Whatever its purpose, I felt empathy for the object as it fumbled along.

Although I made a feeble attempt to make contact through telepathic thoughts, I failed, probably because I don't possess this type of psychic ability. I actually felt disappointed, because I was unable to help.

By now, the proprietor had returned and busied himself, carefully displaying the items on the table for our review. My husband was engaged in conversation with the owner, while I quietly continued to watch as the tiny white orb scurried a few inches off the floor, in the direction of a wall located across the room from where I sat.

I couldn't take my eyes off the bouncing outline of light, for I was mesmerized by the effort this tiny being put forth, in what I assumed was a purposeful intent to investigate the surroundings in which it found itself. If, in fact, the orb did represent a new form of one's existence after death, I wondered how overwhelming this transition must have been?

Upon reaching the wall opposite from where I sat, I was surprised to see the sheetrock had created a roadblock which caused the orb to temporarily oscillate in place, as though in thought. It then appeared to intelligently turn to the right and continue its journey, about three inches off the floor, as it followed the length of the wall to the open doorway. It fluttered along in an erratic circular pattern until it crossed over the threshold, into the hallway, and out of my line of view.

If Disney had created a new Looney Toon cartoon and put the orb's escapades through production, its activities could have been considered comical, were it not for the thought that one day our own spirit might be required to make such a journey alone and afraid.

This experience made me a believer of our spirit's ability to continue an earthly journey, once our essence is outside our mortal body, until we find the spiritual light. It is captivating to think that the energy of the soul is capable of illuminating its way into the darkness, once it is time for the spirit to go beyond the limits of the abilities God has created for mankind.

CHAPTER 27

A Dilemma

My husband had been able to handle his march towards death much better than me, as each step in his downward spiral paved his path toward greater disabilities. About four weeks after our funeral arrangements had been made, the deterioration in his health advanced at a very rapid pace.

His strength weakened due to his lack of nourishment, and it pained me to watch how he could no longer enjoy one of his few remaining simple pleasures, his own independence. Eventually, I accompanied each step he took, ready to grab him as he held onto a walker to steady his once powerful stride. Soon, even this situation became perilous because he began to stumble. For safety reasons, I convinced him to use a wheelchair, which I carefully maneuvered from our bedroom to the front porch, in order to enable him to enjoy the hint of autumn in the air. Now, he was one step closer to losing what little freedom he had previously managed to maintain.

The trees, now sprinkled with tads of yellow and red barely visible within their leaves, were responding to the approaching fall weather by turning color. The leaves would soon start to wither and die, a sign that nature was ending its growing season. My husband's failing health was also an indication that his life cycle was in the process of cessation.

Even his relished enjoyment of the outdoors, though recently limited to the boundary of our front porch, had been whisked away, because suddenly, he was bedridden. The cream-colored walls of our bedroom now replaced God's colorful canvas of nature, and yet somehow, he still managed to smile.

He thanked me each time I placed a mixture of water with icy crystals upon his tongue to quench his thirst. Yet again, another milestone of his journey was reached when even water droplets were unable to provide any relief. Soon, he could no longer swallow the tiniest amount of water without choking.

I was heartbroken when, before my eyes, I watched his transformation from a once healthy man into the epitome of illness, but he never complained. The evolution of the physical deterioration of his strength occurred so quickly, his mental capacity had a hard time catching up with his physical limitations.

At times, he lost track of his disabilities and tried to get out of bed. It was almost like an automatic response to sunshine in the morning. But, quickly, dizziness would alter his course of action, and his head would return to the pillow. I watched him constantly to ensure his safety.

His biggest concern was that he didn't want to burden me. For some reason, he had a hard time grasping the concept that my caring for him was my loving choice and not an assignment. I just wish there was more I could have done to enrich his final days on earth, in order to have made them more enjoyable.

During the night, it had now become impossible for me to sleep because every time I heard him toss or turn, I got up to make sure he was covered and safe.

When I listened for his breathing, I dreaded the thought of the unimaginable day when I would no longer hear this comforting sound.

Although we both were aware the end was near, we didn't discuss the hard reality of death itself. It was extremely difficult to speak of the termination of our relationship as we knew it. Obviously, he knew exactly how I felt, because the one and only time we spoke of our separation due to his impending death, he bared his emotional anxiety in the misty gaze his eyes revealed.

Still, we wouldn't indulge in self-pity, and we never dwelt on the dark side of our situation. It was crucial to remain positive, or else, it would be impossible to function.

The advantage of caring for him at home was obvious. It empowered him to accept his fate and struggle on with life, as though he was at peace with his destiny.

On the other hand, I, too, found solace, but my relief was different than his. Because he was able to rest in the comfort of our bed, and we didn't have to deal with hospital or doctor appointments as a constant reminder of his mortality, I was lulled into the security of a world which concentrated on my positive role as caretaker. Besides, when I rested alongside him, I convinced myself he was just tired or in need of rest . . . while I ignored his fate.

When the time arrived that he was confined to bed, in order to comfort him, I stayed with him day and night, so he knew I was nearby. While I laid in bed, I watched TV during the day and tried, most often unsuccessfully, to sleep during the night. The minute I got up, he would open his eyes and I would hear him say, in a barely audible whisper, "Is everything okay?"

In response to his question, I would walk over, give him a kiss, straighten his covers, and reassure him that I was there.

Because my husband could no longer eat, I, too, had no appetite. I ate food out of necessity in order to maintain my strength. My meals were tiny and quick. My staple was an egg in the morning, and one at night, because I didn't want to cook foods which would emit an aroma to entice his taste buds when they could no longer be satisfied.

My sister and her husband ran all my errands, and I didn't worry about housework or everyday responsibilities, except for the chores which couldn't be put off, like paying bills or feeding the dogs. I knew, in due time, I would have nothing but time on my hands. For the moment, I shared my time with my husband, and cherished what little opportunity we had left to be together.

There was no doubt in my mind, my husband was aware of my presence. I believed he needed me nearby, as a source of security for his unknown journey ahead. Little did he realize how much happiness I derived from the fact that I was the one he sought out to provide sanctuary in his time of need.

One day, after he was bedridden, he woke up and attempted to get out of bed, even though it wasn't safe because he was so weak. I immediately grabbed hold of him and asked, "What are you trying to do?"

Though there appeared to be an urgency to his action, he seemed confused and couldn't explain his reasoning.

While I continued to keep a watchful eye and tried to keep him safe, I began to worry about his sudden limited bouts of energy since it was impossible for me to stay awake 24/7.

Then, one morning, in a matter of seconds, my worst fear came true. After checking my husband and believing him to be asleep, I left the bedroom to get a cup of coffee. I was only halfway down the hall, when I heard a thump. I quickly turned and saw him on the floor, next to our bed, crumpled like a rag doll.

I can only assume that he tried to sit up, got dizzy and passed out. Somehow, he slid down against the mattress, which fortunately helped cushion his fall, because he ended up in a partial sitting position, motionless, with his head down upon his chest.

Overwhelmed with fear, my heart raced as I rushed to his side and knelt down next to him. To prevent him from toppling over any further, I supported his upper body and head in my arms.

At first, I was terrified because I thought he had died. Upon feeling his chest for a heartbeat, I soon realized, although he was unconscious, he was breathing. Thank God, he was still alive! When I held him, I didn't want to let him go, but I knew he needed more than my comforting in this dangerous setting.

Once I assessed the situation and the limited choices available to me, I decided to hold him upright with my left hand and pull the large quilt off the bed with my right. It was heavy, but I found the strength. I then bunched it up around him, to secure him in place. Finally confident that I could let him go, I got up to grab two large pillows off the bed. I propped one under his head and the other on the side of his neck. This way, his airway wouldn't be blocked, and he would be able to breath. I didn't try to move him, or lay him down, because I was uncertain if he had fractured any bones during his fall.

Now, I was faced with a dilemma. He wanted to die at home with me by his side, and not, as he would put it, in a hospital, with stark white walls, in an emotionless setting. I swore to honor his request, but due to his fall, I now worried if my promise might be in jeopardy.

He was already at death's door, and if he had to be transported to the hospital, I knew he would never be allowed to come home again. Unsure of what I should do next, I prayed, "Why did this have to happen now? Please Lord, hasn't he suffered enough already? I beg You Dear Father, don't let him be injured by the fall!"

My prayers must have inspired me, for suddenly, I knew what I needed to do. Believing my husband was currently secure, in his makeshift safety zone, I got up off the floor to call my sister for help. Hearing the anxiety in my voice as I explained the situation, she offered to phone my sister-in-law, who was a retired nurse. We both agreed that she might have a solution. I was grateful for my sister's intervention, for at the moment, all I could think about was to return to my husband's side.

Convinced they would figure out a reasonable plan, I grabbed my cell phone and hurried back to the bedroom to await instructions. No more than a few minutes could have passed, before I reached the bedroom door, when I discovered my husband was now on his side, stretched out on the floor. This encouraged me, because although he looked dazed, he was now semi-conscious and appeared relaxed and comfortable. I now hoped the situation wouldn't be as grim as I first expected.

Without delay, I sat down next to him, lifted his head and placed a pillow underneath for him to rest upon. To keep him warm, I tenderly covered him with our fluffy comforter and began to gently stroke his forehead. This was a familiar technique I often used to relax him, while I soothingly said, "Calm down, everything will be okay." Gradually, he fell into a peaceful sleep.

While my husband rested comfortably, my sister called back to say our sister-in-law suggested that I call an ambulance to request assistance to place a patient back into bed. She also cautioned to be certain to inform the dispatcher that the patient wouldn't be transferred to a facility.

Previously unaware this type of ambulatory service was even available, I followed her advice. After placing the call, I looked down at my husband's fragile body and felt relieved, knowing an ambulance was on its way.

Making sure all the bases were covered, I called the Hospice office as well. I explained the incident and requested a nurse be sent to examine my husband and confirm he wasn't injured.

Now that the wheels of progress were in motion, it was time for me to calm down. I was hopeful my husband's accident would be just an unfortunate incident instead of a major calamity.

By the time we finally reached a moment of quiet peacefulness, our serenity was broken by the shrieking sound of sirens in the distance. And then, the sight of the ambulance pulling down the driveway, with its lights ablaze, soon came into my view.

The spectacle of the paramedics, with determined looks on their faces as they followed me through the doorway, past the kitchen and down the hall, triggered my anxiety anew.

All of the ongoing commotion, a stark contrast from the quiet peaceful moments we just shared, caused my husband to become anxious and confused in his groggy state. Barely able to raise his head off the pillow, he looked up at me. With a look of concern in his eyes, in a soft, weak voice, he invoked my compassion when he said, "You promised me."

Under the circumstances, what else would he think? Since there were now three paramedics and a gurney in our bedroom, he reasoned they were there to take him away.

With every bit of consolation my voice could muster, I encouragingly said, "They are simply here to put you back into bed."

Only once the paramedics appraised the situation, worried about liability, they were apprehensive to lift my husband without knowing if he had any injuries.

I now realized that the resolution of the situation wouldn't be as easy as I had hoped. So, I mustered up my courage to put up a fight and stand my grounds. I firmly stated that it was my husband's right to die at home, and I would respect his wishes.

It appeared my husband wasn't in any pain or discomfort from the fall, and since the paramedics knew a Hospice nurse was on the way, they finally decided to follow my instructions. They agreed to place him back into our bed, but insisted I sign a release of liability first. I couldn't blame them for their concern; however, I was willing to do whatever it took to keep him home for the last few days of his life.

Once our negotiations lead to a satisfactory mutual agreement, another problem arose. How would they manage to get my husband off the floor and into our bed? Normally, a patient is lifted straight up and over onto a gurney. We soon discovered this method wasn't conducive to our current situation.

So, an alternative strategy needed to be put into place. After thoughtful consideration, my husband was carefully lifted onto our blanket. Two paramedics flanked my husband's side of our king-size bed to keep him from falling, while the strongest of the three stood at the bottom of the bed. They all worked in unison as they lifted him up off the floor, at a ninety-degree angle to the bottom right-hand corner of the bed. Once they successfully lifted him onto the bed, two paramedics stayed by his side, while the third one went to the opposite side of the bed. Slowly, so as not to hurt him, they carefully lifted and moved him until they had straightened his position, and now he laid parallel to both sides of the bed. Finally, properly positioned, he was moved inch by inch upward toward the head of the bed. Within a matter of a few minutes, he had been put comfortably back into place.

While the turmoil of moving my husband was underway, the Hospice nurse arrived. Once he was securely in place, the male nurse asked everyone to leave the room, so he could examine my husband in private. A few minutes later, he emerged from our bedroom to confirm my husband hadn't been injured during his fall.

The bustling noises from the paramedics, who had been chatting in the kitchen while they awaited confirmation all was well, returned to silence once I escorted them out the door. Instantly, all was quiet. Only stillness existed, while the nurse and I were left to look after my husband.

As I proceeded down the hall to join the nurse in our bedroom, I was overcome by sadness. I felt it was my fault that my husband had been subjected to this turmoil. While he slept, I discussed my concern about the possibility of his falling again, so the nurse showed me how to fix the bed to keep my husband safe. The nurse set pillows under the sheets, at the right-side edge of the bed, which created a cushioned dam to protect him.

A short time later, once the nurse was satisfied my husband was asleep, he suggested we go to the kitchen and talk. He spoke softly and caringly while we discussed my husband's physical transition process, and the nurse explained how the body lacked the need for food or water . . . as death drew near.

He assured me that my husband's body would no longer require the nourishment it formerly needed to provide life. He spent a considerable amount of time with me, because he wanted to make sure I understood that my husband's time was limited . . . a few days at most.

I appreciated his kind words and caring concern for my husband as well as for me.

Finally, I heard a solemnness in his voice when he apprehensively, almost apologetically, told me he had asked my husband, "Are you afraid to die?"

He wanted me to know my husband wasn't afraid. I nodded my head in acknowledgement, and with a sincere smile, replied, "I know."

Once he believed he had accomplished his mission of mercy as both nurse and comforter, he reluctantly left me to my destiny.

With everyone gone, I understood the final stages of my husband's life were underway. Now, that I was alone with my husband and my thoughts, I heard the silence and felt the solitude his death would soon release upon my heart.

CHAPTER 28

"When You See the Light, Go to It, For I Will Find You There"

As my husband's health declined, so did my happiness. There was no denying the evidence, his time was drawing dangerously near as the yellowing of the whites of his eyes betrayed his fate. Tuesday's events had reinforced the fact that he was now approaching death's door.

My heart was broken. I was torn between my selfish desire to have him hold onto life for my sake, and my loving compassion for him to no longer have to suffer. I wondered how I would handle the daunting task which now consumed me. He will die in our bed, and I alone will be there to bear witness to his passing. Would I have the courage to face this difficult part of our journey by myself?

Although the scales had finally tipped, and his illness was now on the verge of winning the war, he hadn't let his illness interfere with his ability to find contentment in the smallest of places. In the past few weeks, each time he encountered another downhill milestone along his journey, he took it in stride, without objection.

Toward the end of his life, on the few occasions he had been able to sustain a brief conversation with me, there was always a calmness in his voice. Somehow, he still managed to provide a smile, along with a "Thank you," for the only fluid he was now able to enjoy . . . a moist sponge to wet his lips.

When he fell the other day, the nurse showed me how to administer morphine, through a measured eyedrop style dispenser, which calmed him and helped him sleep. In his last few days, although he didn't complain of pain, he became restless when the medication started to wear off, and I could tell he was very uncomfortable because of his constant fidgeting.

Due to his significant weight loss, his body was now ice cold all of the time. His relentless tossing and turning, during the past few days, continually jumbled the blankets, and it became a constant effort to keep him covered.

As the end was nearing, my husband would become extremely agitated, as though he was in a fight for his life. Then, amazingly, during the night, he amassed enough strength to pull himself up, as though he intended to get out of bed again. Instantaneously, I put my arm around his waist to stop his movement. Due to the fact his former strength had declined significantly, I was able to keep him in place. From experience, I knew this burst of energy represented a transitional phase, but I still wasn't ready to let him go.

While holding him, I calmly asked, "What's wrong?"

In a faint voice, he replied, "I have to get up."

When I lovingly told him, "There is no reason for you to get out of bed," he calmed down. Then, I held him and caringly ran my fingers thought his hair, hoping to lull him back to sleep.

Knowing the opportunity to express my cherished affection for my husband was coming to an end, I affectionately said, "I love you." Though he was extremely weak, I fondly remember his tender response, "I love you too."

For some unknown reason, I began to feel as though my husband's time was nearing, and an emotional struggle began to develop within me as I continued to hold him in my arms.

At first I thought, please don't leave me . . . not yet. But, due to the illumination of the moonlight which encompassed our room, there was enough light for me to see an expression of confusion begin to overshadow his face . . . instead of the peaceful sleep I had hoped for.

This worried me even more, for I knew certain people, as they neared death, see visions of family members coming to guide them on their final journey home.

Before my father died, I was present when he displayed a puzzled expression upon his face. As he looked up at the ceiling, my father clearly asked, why were his mother and brothers (who were deceased) in his room? At the time of his death, my father had advanced Alzheimer's disease and had been unable to speak in logical sentences for quite some time. Yet, as my father approached his death, he conveyed his thoughts quite clearly.

Thinking about my father's reaction during his transitional period into the next life, and anticipating that my husband might express some form of otherworldly acknowledgement if he was nearing death at this particular moment, I looked into his eyes for evidence he might be witnessing some form of spiritual manifestation, but there was none.

Wondering if my husband's mind was fixated upon a journey he expected to make, which might explain the urgency in his attempt to get up, I took it upon myself to examine the ceiling of our bedroom for some form of mystical sign I might detect which could be an indication of his imminent passing.

Although I hadn't expected to see anything, as I searched the ceiling in every corner of our room, I was amazed to see two beautiful bright orange orbs, about an inch and a half in diameter, with dark halos encircling each sphere. They were hovering next to each other, near the ceiling, to the left of the master bedroom's open door.

Spellbound by these manifestations and in awe of their color, I momentarily stared at them. When I was finally able to break my startled gaze, I looked down at my husband to see if he was aware of their presence. Because he faced the opposite direction, he showed no sign of acknowledgement of their existence. When I quickly looked back up, they were gone. This interaction led me to believe, I was the one appointed to receive the message that his time was near, and soon his suffering would end.

Believing my notion was reasonably correct but still unprepared to release my embrace upon my husband's soul from his earthly ties, a soothing thought entered my mind. My sister had recently read a book about the journey of our souls. She was fascinated by the author's concept that a small portion of each person's soul remained in heaven when the spirit of life was created in the womb. In addition, she abstractly alleged that the author claimed, when identical twins were conceived, each twin's soul came to earth leaving a full half of their soul in heaven, though she said the author was unable to unequivocally explain why.

Although I hadn't read the book, being an identical twin, I was captivated by the concept. So I chose this moment to look up to heaven and reflect on the notion, thinking hypothetically, "If it is true that half of my soul remained in heaven, I ask you (imploring to the other half of my own soul) to please come for him (my husband), because he will know you, and he will go to you."

Suddenly, I realized, by requesting a spiritual guide for my husband's soul, I had released him from his earthly bonds since I had finally accepted the imminence of his death. I felt a powerful sensation of hope, while I silently prayed for his salvation.

Then, I whispered into my husband's ear, "Go to the light! Don't stay in the darkness . . . for you won't find me in the darkness. When you see the light, go to it, for I will find you there. Don't worry about me, I will be okay. Go to the light!"

At that moment, I felt his body completely relax, and he finally fell into a peaceful sleep. It was the most comfortable I had seen him in a long time. So, as he slept, I got up and covered him . . . one last time.

CHAPTER 29

The Sensation in the Room
Was of Peaceful Bliss

Sleep had eluded me for some time now. My constant vigils during the nights, to make sure my husband was safe and secure, were taking their toll on me. I was exhausted, both physically, as well as mentally. Yet, for some reason, last night was different.

I will never forget the sense of calm which permeated throughout our bedroom after we exchanged the affectionate expression of the love we still shared, and I encouraged my husband to search out the light by reassuring him that I would find him in our next life.

As a result of our caring exchange, a peaceful rest enveloped my husband, and it was magical. It felt as though some invisible power had taken over the stress and problems in his life, and he no longer had to struggle to survive.

The sound of his restful breathing produced a calming effect which suddenly allowed me to fall into a relaxed sleep . . . once I sensed that I had been granted a temporary relief from my own suffering as well.

Four hours passed, in what seemed like minutes, and now it was time for me to administer my husband's next dose of morphine. It was still dark when I got up. While I looked over at my husband, in the shadowy haze of our bedroom, I was happy to see he appeared to be quietly resting, so I thanked God for His kindness. All of a sudden, I felt the sensation of a peaceful bliss, and it was extremely exhilarating. I actually took in a deep breath, as though I might be able to ingest the ecstasy I felt. At that moment, I associated my happiness with my husband's serenity.

Wanting him to enjoy his sleep for a little while longer, I quietly headed into the kitchen to carefully measure out the minimum dosage of morphine which was now due.

Since the sun had not risen as of yet, when I returned to our bedroom, I used the dimmer switch to slowly control the brightness of the lights, to waken him but not startle him in the process. Once my eyes became accustomed to the soft glow of the overhead recessed lighting, I suddenly had a strange inclination that something was wrong.

It took a few seconds for me to realize, he wasn't in his normal sleeping position. He was on his back; he never slept on his back.

Once I saw his face, I took a closer look and suddenly, my eyes were drawn to his. In the dim lighting, they didn't look normal. They were partially open, had a shiny glaze and appeared blackish in color. Finally, as my gaze slowly drifted towards his mouth, I noticed, it too was open, in a fixed position.

That was when I realized, for the first time, he was no longer resting . . . he had died.

Then, as if in a trance, I slowly walked over to confirm my observations.

As I leaned over him, there was no movement. I could feel the coldness emitting from his face, as stiffness met the gentle kiss I placed upon his lips, to say my last goodbye. Since I had kept him covered, his body was still warm, so I assumed it hadn't been long since his spirit had departed its earthly host.

Although his body no longer contained the soul which gave him life, I felt his loving presence around me. And now, after the realization of his death, I believed the peaceful bliss I had previously felt was a feeling of love his spirit emitted.

Mixed emotions swept over me. I was torn between my grief and my obligation to perform the difficult duties which lay ahead. So, I took time to sit down next to him and remember the wonderful life we enjoyed together before I set the funeral wheels in motion. While I sat, I said a silent prayer to God for mercy and spiritual guidance for his soul during his journey home.

When I looked down upon his lifeless body, I suddenly realized the care I gave him had helped me in return; because the compassion we have for the suffering of others, and the effort we put forth to relieve our loved one's distress, provides a God-given gratification beyond explanation.

Now that my job as caretaker had ended, it was time to tackle the difficult preparations for his funeral. I slowly collected my strength and called my sister. She and her husband were on their way.

Since my husband and I hadn't attended church for many years, my next call was to my niece, who dutifully attended the church where my husband and I were registered in name only. I had previously alerted her to my husband's approaching need for a priest, and she was the one who graciously made these arrangements.

Considering all of the calls I made that morning, the one to my daughter was the most difficult. Even though she knew her father's death was imminent, her sobbing voice exposed the pent-up sorrow only time would heal.

My sister and her husband pulled down the driveway while I talked to my daughter on the phone. A few minutes later, my niece and the Monsignor arrived, and I led our small solemn gathering into the bedroom, where my husband's service for his Last Rites would be performed. While the Monsignor led us in prayer, I bowed my head in reverence to God, which helped hide my tears of sadness.

During our period of meditation, my sister's attention was captivated by the flickering of the overhead lights I had turned on to assist Monsignor in his religious readings. She became fascinated with the thought that my husband was trying to get my attention, to let me know he had reached the other side.

Actually, I didn't want to be presumptuous and validate this line of thought. Besides, I couldn't confirm the occurrence since I wasn't looking up at the time to witness the event.

Even though my husband had experienced paranormal anomalies while he was alive, which included following a shadow figure through an empty house while I was present and hearing disembodied voices at a home we once owned, we never discussed the notion of trying to make spiritual contact after one of us had died. The idea that either one of us should attempt such a feat never came up in any of our conversations. So, at that moment, I wasn't convinced my sister's interpretation of the flickering lights during Monsignor's blessings was plausible.

Upon completion of my husband's prayer service, the five of us returned to the kitchen. My sister and I began to carry on a friendly discussion with the Monsignor about our families' religious beliefs and internal spiritual relationship with God when suddenly, the six bulbs in the kitchen dinette light fixture started to vigorously flicker on and off. At this moment, there was no denying the event occurred. As a matter of fact, you could have heard a pin drop while we all stared in amazement, until the anomaly stopped of its own accord a short time thereafter.

Looking to the Monsignor for guidance, he acknowledged the phenomenon, stating he was not surprised. He explained that he was aware of many similar spiritual events which had taken place as a result of the death of a loved one. He suggested, as time passed, I should expect other unexplained activities to occur as well.

In the Monsignor's opinion, the activities would heighten during the early grieving process, but as time passed and my grief moderated, the events would lessen, though possibly, they might never completely end. Since I now had faith this new experience, involving the flickering lights, demonstrated a validation in my belief of the continuation of our soul's essence after death, his words inspired me. It was exciting to interpret the event as proof the spirit of my husband's soul lived on.

The unexplained anomaly had brought our conversation to an abrupt conclusion, and since it was Friday, the 2nd of October, a work day for both the Monsignor and my niece, they had to leave to continue on with their busy daily schedules.

Shortly after they left, my daughter and her husband arrived, and the rest of my day would be filled with the normal activities one must endure while struggling through the funeral process.

Throughout the morning, while my husband's body laid in wait for his journey to the funeral home, his physical presence still provided me with a sense of his existence.

By the time the funeral director arrived to pick up his body and his clothes, which were carefully chosen by my daughter and me, it was decided that a showing would take place on Sunday and the funeral would be scheduled for Monday.

Now, there were flowers to order and the repass meal to confirm, until suddenly, as though the world had stopped, there were no more decisions to make. The activities of the day had kept me busy, with little time left for me to absorb the tragic event which had just destroyed my life. By the end of the day, when I returned home, our empty house seemed to echo with sounds of sorrow that his absence had created.

Though I knew my family was dealing with the same loss, separation anxiety and grief I felt, they didn't understand the overwhelming heartache which overtook me. I believed, in time, life would eventually return to normal for everyone else, but not for me. The happiness I once shared with my husband . . . his touch, his kiss and his embrace was now beyond my mortal reach. I was devastated!

My sister and her husband offered to stay for a while, to keep me company on my first night alone, but I declined their caring invitation. I hugged and thanked them both for all their sympathetic support. At the moment, although I was a lost soul, what I needed most was time and solitude, in order to find my own way out of the darkness.

They understood my sentiment and left me to face my grief alone. I watched the tail lights of their car slowly fade away, as they drove down the path heading toward the road. When I locked the door and slowly proceeded to the kitchen, a feeling of desolation swept over me.

I thought about the progression of my husband's death and how people died every day, but not until today did I ever understand how the survivor actually felt. Now, under the circumstances, I finally could identify with how deep a loss is suffered by the one who is left behind.

CHAPTER 30

While I Prayed for His Salvation, My Heart Ached for His Presence

There was now a loneliness which hung over me, and it existed whether I was alone or with other people. The feeling was a complete transformation from the gratification I had just recently felt while I cared for my husband during the final weeks of his life.

Now, the fear of being alone and the emptiness I felt, over the loss of the relationship I so joyfully shared with husband, consumed me. Grief held me in its grasp, and I suddenly fell into the depths of despair and found myself not caring if I lived or died.

While I wandered through the empty rooms of our home, I searched for some feeling of hope, but it completely eluded me. The only peace I found was in prayer, however, it didn't last long enough for me to find any permanent comfort.

Evening approached, and as the dusk of nightfall engulfed the farthest reaches of my bedroom, I had to face the anguish I had dreaded all day. I must spend my first night alone, knowing my husband would never return.

As I prepared for bed, I went into our closet, took one of my husband's knit shirts and put it on . . . since this was all I had left to comfort me. Once I settled in for the night, my heart ached for his presence.

It wasn't easy to sleep while I wondered how I would get through the next three days. I was overwhelmed by the thought of all the people I must greet, and I questioned if I would be able to hold up a facade of strength when my fortitude had been crippled by a fact of life we all must endure.

Throughout the night, I constantly woke up to listen for the comforting sounds of my husband's breathing, only to realize he was no longer with me. This new silence would become a relentless reminder that I was alone, since now, my sobbing was the only sound I would hear.

When I woke up the next morning to the sight of my husband's empty side of the bed, I was again jolted into the realization that death had taken him from me. I felt as though I was in a nightmare from which I hoped to awaken. It would take a long time before this new reality settled in and I would be able to greet the morning light without having to daily relive the event of his death.

Though not by choice, today was the beginning of a new life for me, and I wasn't happy about it at all. Uncertainty awaited me at every corner I turned, for it had been a long time since I had to face life's challenges alone.

I dwelt in self-pity throughout the day . . . until finally, I found some consolation in the fact that I wasn't the first person alive to lose their loved one . . . and I definitely wouldn't be the last.

CHAPTER 31

The Calling Hours

While I agonized over the loss of my husband and dealt with the slow passage of time in anticipation of the funeral services which lay ahead, the next two days were extremely painful. No matter how difficult it was to struggle through the daylight hours, my nights were unbearable. After the many loving years we had shared together, I was tortured by the thought of waking up each morning alone in our bed. This seemed to be an insurmountable obstacle for me to overcome.

Each night, in-between the few moments of fidgety sleep I managed to achieve, I anxiously awoke filled with the fear I had fallen asleep and my husband needed me, only to suddenly realize he had died. At these moments of renewed awareness, I broke down all over again, in an onslaught of tears. My nights became a carousel of sweet anticipation of waking to his kiss, followed by the desperation I felt at the awareness of my loss.

How will I live on when life no longer has a meaning, was the thought constantly on my mind.

As I searched my wardrobe for the appropriate clothing to match my broken heart, there was no longer any color in my life. Shades of black and grey were all I sought to appease my grief-stricken heart, so prior to retiring for the evening, I carefully laid out my black suit for the following day's events.

When early morning arrived, the time had come for me to get up, shower and dress for the difficult day ahead. Although my actions were robotic in nature, as though some unforeseen force controlled each step I took, I was overpowered with a perception of emptiness and wondered if I would ever be able to escape this feeling of despair?

Everything I thought or did reminded me of my husband. How I longed for the sound of his voice, the touch of his hand on mine, or the smile on his face. I felt lost and abandoned. During moments like this, the only strength I could muster was through my faith in God, so I prayed for help to get me through the next few days.

No matter how distraught I felt emotionally, at least for the time being I had a purpose, though it was a sorrowful one. Of course, in few hours I would be comforted by family and friends at the funeral home, but the thought of facing so many people in my fragile emotional state was unsettling.

After I dressed and nibbled on breakfast, it wasn't long before my daughter, my sister and their husbands arrived.

In order to calm my nerves before heading to the funeral home, we all gathered in the kitchen to spend a few minutes on small talk. It was during this conversation when I began to analyze a string of coincidental irregularities which had started to stack up.

My trail of events began when I first entered the kitchen that morning, turned on the recessed lights and one of the ceiling lights blew out.

Then, while in the kitchen with my family, I opened the refrigerator door to get something to drink and heard a pop. The interior light bulb just failed.

Next, when I walked into the attached garage, where the replacement bulbs were kept, I smiled when I noticed a florescent ceiling light no longer worked.

Finally, once I returned to the kitchen, my daughter announced she had difficulties with her iPhone. Somehow the curser, all by itself, typed in letters in the search box, and she had no control over her phone. She quickly showed the rest of us the odd phenomena before it finally stopped. She was pleased, since she interpreted this unusual event as her father's way of letting her know he was thinking of her.

It had suddenly become apparent to all of us, that my husband's spirit had quickly learned how to attract our attention.

In time, in addition to his ability to blow light bulbs and interfere with cell phone usage, his spirit became proficient at the use of other electrical devices. For now, it appeared as though these events were just the start of many coincidental spirited activities which continued to amuse my daughter, my sister and me for some time to come.

Although we had been engaged in a pleasant conversation regarding my husband's apparent attempts to contact us, we soon realized it was time to head to the funeral home for the showing, or we would be late.

Everyone followed my cue, gathered their belongings and began to proceed to their cars. After I let my family out through the office exterior door, all I needed to do was retrace my steps back through the room, turn on the alarm at the mud room door, and exit the house into the garage. Then, we should have been on our way.

Instead of executing this simple procedure, once I locked the door, turned around, and took my first few steps, I suddenly felt a crippling pain rush throughout my lower foot. When I tried to figure out what had just triggered my agony, I looked down and saw my husband's walker lying next to my injured ankle. Although I hadn't passed anywhere near it, somehow the walker had fallen over, hitting my outer ankle bone, which caused it to start to swell.

Unable to walk, or even stand without agonizing pain, I hobbled over to the office door, opened it, and called out for help.

Once aware something must be seriously wrong because of the sound of the alarm in my voice, everyone piled back into the office wondering what the commotion was all about. The sight of my ankle, clearly visible through my shear stockings, swelling and turning black and blue as we all watched, confused my family, especially since it took no more than a few seconds for the whole event to transpire.

Within a short period of time, the aching and throbbing grew to unbearable proportions. I wondered if I needed to go to the hospital. Then again, how could I possibly go since I was expected at the funeral home in less than half an hour?

Obviously, I was in extreme agony, but there was no time to do anything about it. After careful inspection, we all agreed it didn't appear as though anything was broken.

Only now, because I had been wearing a skirt, suit jacket and high heels, I needed to change my clothes and find a way to secure and support my badly swollen ankle, so I could function. I finally determined that the best thing to do was to stuff my injured foot into a boot in order to prevent further swelling.

So, the culprit which caused my injury, now became my salvation. I used the walker to get to my bedroom, changed into slacks, wrapped my ankle with an ACE bandage, put on a pair of socks, and found a pair of boots to fit over my severely swollen, bandaged ankle. It took a few tries before I finally decided upon the one and only pair that would do the trick.

Precious moments were lost during the fiasco but, according to our original plans, we had initially allocated enough extra time to enable us to still get to the funeral home without being late.

When finally en route, we all decided it would be best if I used a wheelchair at the funeral home to get inside the building, but the funeral director was confused when we arrived and my sister requested one. Once I emerged from the car and struggled to stand, as I held onto the walker for support, he quickly sent an assistant to fetch one.

I was able to keep a better frame of mind, while I waited for the wheelchair to arrive, by kidding with the proprietor about my lightbulb scenarios.

Since he and my husband had created a bond of friendship while my husband was still alive, he smiled and then joked, "I can see your husband doing such things from the other side."

After being seated, I was rolled into the funeral home's viewing area. It had been a little over 48 hours since I last saw my husband's body. I got up and struggled to make my way up to the casket, where I reached for my husband's hand to gently touch it. Even though his hand was cold, it warmed my heart as wonderful memories flowed through my mind.

Because of the pain I felt when I tried to move my foot, I knew it was impossible for me to constantly get up from a sitting position to greet my family and friends. So, instead of using the cushioned high-back chair which had been set out for me, I requested a high stool instead. The support of the taller stool allowed me to alternately stand on my good foot, or sit on the stool, while welcoming my guests. Although I was in terrible pain, I did my best to ignore the physical aspect of my agony, since I had more than I could handle dealing with the mental stress I was currently under. I got through the showing by concentrating on the outpouring of sympathy from the caring people in attendance, which unexpectedly provided a desperately needed feeling of well-being.

Once the calling hours had ended and I found myself at home alone, I was saddened by the prospect of the morning light. Tomorrow my husband's casket would be closed forever, and then, only his memory would remain in my heart.

CHAPTER 32

The Funeral

By morning, as I lay in bed, the pain radiating from my ankle was overpowering. For this reason, I tried to stay motionless throughout the night because the slightest amount of movement caused aching and throbbing, which immediately escalated into a sharp, stabbing pain. Instead of the overnight improvement I had hoped for, the swelling hardened and displayed signs of a long recovery.

It was time for me to rise, so I carefully sat up and lifted my injured leg over the side of my bed. The resulting pressure, of the blood running down to my ankle, created an unpleasant warmth in the area of my injury. At least, by that point, it was a welcome relief to know I could tolerate the pain.

Afraid to put any weight on the injured area, I took hold of the walker I had placed on the side of my bed the night before, for easy access. When I tried to stand on my good leg, I soon discovered the slightest transfer of weight onto my swollen ankle resulted in crippling pain.

In order to get around, I found it was necessary for me to place some pressure on my bruised ankle. Shooting pain was my body's way of telling me this wasn't a good idea. Since necessity is the mother of invention, I realized the only way I could reach my bathroom, to get ready for the challenging day ahead, was to support my upper body by holding onto the walker while I hopped along on my good foot.

I now grasped the reality of my situation; this would be a rough day, in more ways than one.

After I conquered my first dilemma of the day, I dressed and then determined I could barely fit my swollen ankle into my boot, which had supported it the day before. After repeated attempts, I was finally able to zip up the side of my boot, but only after I suffered through the pain of forcing my foot into place.

Dealing with the difficulties my injury had created was just an added inconvenience. It paled in comparison to my zombie-like approach to life. To say I felt like the walking dead was an understatement.

Every action I needed to make was a forced one, because I was living my life in a fog, not knowing up from down. I couldn't concentrate or think about what tomorrow might bring, much less comprehend what I needed to do next. Although on the outside I might have looked normal, on the inside I was a mess.

Then, out of nowhere, my husband's words reached my inner conscience, "You are a strong woman, and I have always been proud of you because of it."

Encouraged by this inspiration, I thought about how many people, on a daily basis, experience what I was about to face. So, with God's help, I managed to find the strength to fight my battle against self-pity, ever mindful of the fact that God still had a purpose for me, and that was why my life must go on.

With the added problems I had to deal with that morning because of my injury, before I knew it, my family arrived to bring me to the funeral home. This time, there wasn't time for chit-chat since the funeral mass was scheduled for 10 AM, and we needed to be at the funeral home before the casket was closed and brought to the church.

Upon reaching the parking lot, the funeral director assisted me out of the vehicle, with a sheepish look on his face. While he helped me into the wheelchair, he said he had something special for me. He smiled when he placed a light bulb into my hand and explained that the ceiling light had popped when he switched on the lights in the showing room in anticipation of our arrival. Remembering my story about the bulbs blowing at my house, he saved the bulb for me as a memento.

He wanted me to know that my husband was playing games at his establishment as well. I believe this was the proprietor's way to cheer me up and help me through the difficult funeral process I was about to face. I appreciated the humor of the situation, and it definitely helped lift my spirits.

Following our light-hearted conversation, the five of us were permitted to spend time in the viewing room for our final private moments before my husband's coffin would be sealed forever.

Once my sister, daughter and their husbands said their last farewells, I limped up to the casket and tenderly kissed my husband goodbye.

Tears flowed down my cheeks as I was wheeled out of the room, and I brokenheartedly looked back at the casket whispering, *I love you,* for only him to hear.

Our small group was now escorted to the limo where we sat and waited for the coffin to be brought out to the hearse, prior to our procession to the church. Once we were on our way, even though my family was with me, I was consumed by loneliness during the short ride.

Due to the fact my husband and I didn't request a showing at the funeral home for the morning of the funeral, my family and friends were already gathered at the church awaiting our arrival. After our limo was parked, I emerged and took a deep breath before I struggled to maneuver my way into the wheelchair. It was difficult to look at the hearse behind me, knowing my husband's body would be buried before the end of the day.

While I was wheeled down the church aisle to the front row seat, I knew it wasn't an envious position to be in. As I watched the flag-draped casket being reverently rolled along side of me, my mind was flooded with recollections of our early relationship.

The flag brought back memories of the period of time my husband spent in Vietnam. Thank God, he was one of the lucky ones who made it home, thus allowing us to share so many wonderful years together. Throughout the years, I often felt anguish for the families who weren't as fortunate.

When the Monsignor began the funeral mass, as though snapped out of a pleasant dream, sadness quickly replaced my happy memories. After the gospel reading, the Monsignor eloquently spoke about my husband's life, death, family and his eternal salvation.

Knowing the heart-wrenching tribute that was to follow, I braced myself for my brother-in-law's kind and loving words when the time for the eulogy arrived. As he fought to control his own emotions, his witty remarks and carefully chosen reflection upon my husband's life brought tears to many eyes in church that day.

Once the funeral mass ended, our procession headed to the cemetery where a military funeral, with uniformed Marines and a 21-gun salute, awaited me.

The accumulation of the day's events finally broke down my defenses, and my emotions could no longer be contained. While my daughter and sister were flanked on each side of me, holding my hand for moral support, nothing could hold back my tears of sorrow.

After the final prayers were completed and the guns were fired, a lone Marine knelt down in front of me to respectfully present the American Flag. During this tribute, I also felt the loss so many military families have experienced throughout history. Even though my husband didn't die during the Vietnam War, he died as a result of it. Although my heart was broken, I was proud to be counted among the patriotic families whose loved ones served their country by making their ultimate sacrifice. The ceremony made me feel as though his Brothers and Sisters, who served along with him, were there in spirit, and in respect of his memory.

After the gravesite ceremony ended, I spoke with the few remaining people who lingered to extend their deepest sympathy and apologized for being unable to join me for the post-funeral reception.

Now that the cemetery had finally emptied, except for the lone limo which awaited me for my final ride, I was allowed to sit alone, for my own moment of private reflection, to say my final goodbye.

CHAPTER 33

The Post-Funeral Luncheon

When we drove out of the cemetery, along with my husband's body, I left my heart behind. Now, I had to pick up the pieces and try to make some sense out of what God wanted me to do with the rest of my life. At the moment, I didn't have a clue.

The only thing I knew for certain was that we were on our way to partake in the post-funeral luncheon to conclude the funeral process.

Since both the mass and cemetery ceremonies had been exceptionally difficult to endure, I was grateful to have had some time to compose myself along the way. The luncheon was important to me, for it gave me a chance to thank everyone for their loving support, and I looked forward to that opportunity.

By the time we drove into the parking lot, it was already full. Fortunately, a parking space had been saved in front of the restaurant door, which made it easier for me to maneuver my way into the dining area. When I entered the room, the smell of fresh brewed coffee and the chatter of friendly voices enveloped the open dining space. China coffee cups, water glasses, silverware, and hand linens were set out on top of the white tablecloths, which covered the round tables strategically set throughout the room.

Warm food had been laid out on a buffet table to satisfy the hearty appetites of those who had already gathered into cozy groups, socializing amongst themselves at the individual tables. The aroma of the freshly prepared food was inviting, once the tray tops were removed and the entrees were ready to be served. The camaraderie shared by all, during the luncheon, turned an extremely stressful day into a pleasant afternoon.

Time passed quickly. The dinner plates were cleared, dessert was served and the time had come for my family and friends to head back to their normal weekday activities. Then, everyone who attended made a point to stop by my table before they left, to repeat their heartfelt condolences and reassuring departing words, for which I was extremely grateful.

Soon the room had emptied, except for my small supportive group of four, and the friendly chatter, which had just recently resonated throughout the room, was quickly replaced by a feeling of confusion that suddenly came over me.

During the time of the luncheon, the sounds of laughter, the sights of familiar faces, and the noisy dining room activities had somehow managed to quiet the storm of sadness inside of me, at least for the hour or so it took for the dining to transpire.

Isolation traded places with the recent bustle of activities, and for some reason, I suddenly felt lonely. Then, I looked around in anticipation, searching . . . somewhat expecting my husband to walk up behind me, like so many times before, to tell me it was time for us to go home. When I realized my search was in vain, it was a grim reminder of my loss.

So, when my sister approached me to suggest the remaining food should be wrapped up to take with us, I was perplexed and unresponsive. Though I had heard her words, I couldn't comprehend what she had said. Instead of an acknowledgement, a look of confusion was my response.

Seeing the dismay in my face, my sister took control. She immediately ordered the staff to box up the food, especially, since the day before she had looked in my refrigerator and noticed it was empty.

Her observation was correct. Food hadn't been a high priority on my list of necessities, and my desire to eat regular meals again would come slowly.

After the food was boxed and placed in the cars, even though I felt relief the trying events of the funeral were behind me, I was bewildered by the thought of where my life was headed. All the carefully laid out plans my husband and I had prepared together were now complete, and it would be up to me to take my next steps on my own.

My sister then came over to me to say it was time for us to leave. With a smile, she said I should hobble my way to their car, so they could take me home. I followed her instructions like a lost child, for that is exactly how I felt.

When we got home, my sister and daughter wrapped all of the food in individual servings and put them in the freezer, to alleviate their worries that I wouldn't have anything to eat.

Since my daughter and her husband had to work full-time jobs, my sister and her husband happily stepped up to the plate and stood behind their vow to my husband to look after me.

In the days, weeks, months and even years to come, family played an important role in getting my life back in order.

My sister's perception of my helplessness, especially during the period of my ankle rehabilitation, was right on the mark. She and her husband became beacons of light in my darkness, for I was a ship floundering at sea, in need of guidance from the stability of an on-shore lighthouse, until my ballasts could someday be stabilized to create a time when my grief would be contained and hopefully overcome.

CHAPTER 34

I No Longer Had a Purpose in Life

Nothing could have prepared me for the loneliness I suffered after my husband's death. Now that the funeral was over, it seemed I no longer had a purpose in life. I was a lost soul in need of direction. So I pleaded for guidance from God.

The activities surrounding the funeral process helped fill some of my lonely hours, but once I completed the ceremonies associated with my husband's death, it became agonizingly evident that without his presence I no longer had any interest in life itself. Although I realized going forward wouldn't be easy, I never dreamed it would be so hard.

At times, I wondered if I didn't have the responsibility to attend to the needs of my pets would I have chosen to ignore my own well-being? The obligation I felt to attend to their needs, influenced my duty to care for myself as well. If the dogs had to eat, then so did I. Therefore, my maternal instincts kicked in, and I looked after us all.

Within a week, my ankle was on the mend, but my physical pain wasn't my real issue. I often wondered, would I ever be happy again? Would the day come when I woke up in the morning without experiencing a repetition of the emotional distress I suffered through the day before?

At least in the movie, *Groundhog Day,* Bill Murry learned a lesson before his next morning's revival began anew.

Eventually, like Bill, I also got the message. I learned that I needed to adjust to getting up, eating breakfast, reading the newspaper, accomplishing everyday activities I had always performed; only now, I did them alone. It may sound ridiculous that I had to adjust to performing these ordinary endeavors, but every mundane activity I completed made me feel as though something was missing.

That important something was my husband who, because of his presence, had always made these ordinary, everyday activities extraordinary for me. There is a huge difference between sharing your dreams, discussing your problems, taking a walk, talking over coffee, or simply going for a ride with someone you love, versus doing them alone. Compared to how much change had taken place in my life, these examples were a drop in the hat.

What I found astonishing, as I began my journey of grief, was how different my perception of normal would become. During the time my husband was alive, my positive vision structured my life's journey. Despite the fact that life had its way of throwing a monkey wrench at us, in-between periods of contentment, I never felt as though the weight of the world laid upon my shoulders alone, as I knew it did now.

Once grief entered into the picture, I believe my brain created a protection mode which tried to block out everything . . . the good, as well as the bad. It became a real effort to think or make decisions. I actually felt as though I had entered into a period of early Alzheimer's disease because I was confused about every decision I needed to make.

At that time, I was no longer the person who could multi-task from morning till night, the person I used to be. Suddenly, I was unable to choose what I would make for supper. For that matter, I couldn't decide when it was time to eat. A feeling of helplessness became my new normal existence, and it was incredibly frustrating.

As a result of my devastating loss, grief had also stolen my personality. My heart had been swallowed by my anguish, and I needed to find a way to climb my way out of the depths

186

of despair. I learned how dark the world could be, even when the sun was shining and the birds were singing, because their love songs were wasted on me. Contentment became a word without meaning.

It would take a while before I would understand exactly how grief's negativity affected me. Psychologically speaking, I understood the definition of the word grief, I just didn't expect the consequences that came along as its baggage.

In order to take my *first step forward,* I needed to accept God's will. My *next major challenge* would be to figure out how I would overcome my grief, even though I had no idea how long the process would take.

In time, my desire to conquer the dread I faced each morning would have beneficial effects. Although my grief didn't instantaneously evaporate, I slowly felt encouraged as I became acclimated to the fact that even though I was unhappy with my circumstances, I was capable of living on my own.

After my loss, I had to take things slowly because my brain had locked down and I didn't have the key. Comparatively speaking, the body's way of responding to injury is to redirect its energy to promote healing of the wound. So too, my brain needed calming from the injury inflicted against it by my suffering, which resulted in my mind shutting down its ability to function. Therefore, I had to overcome my inability to think. I felt as though my brain had gone on vacation, leaving an empty void during its leave of absence. As hard as I tried to contemplate the next step I needed to take to get my life in order, my mind was confused and didn't want to perform its normal thought processes. It was annoying, to say the least. To overcome my *first hurdle,* I slowly established a new pattern, a new normal for me to live by. That meant I needed to get accustomed to a structured daily schedule, just like before; only now, I would have to complete my daily activities alone. Once my mind accepted this new normal, it became more receptive to tackling other new ideas.

I could tell by the way my brain was currently functioning, there wouldn't be a return to normal anytime soon. So, I didn't fret about what I couldn't do, I just worked towards accomplishing what I could get done, one issue at a time.

My *second hurdle* was how to deal with my emotional roller coaster ride while in public. At this fragile time in my life, my home was the only place I felt safe and protected against the sadness I encountered each time I had to deal with the sporadic condolences from the good-hearted people I met at the store. Although I wouldn't let seclusion take over my life forever, in order to heal my grief, I understood I still needed time to adjust to my loss.

In my limited capacity, I knew the answer to healing my sadness didn't lie in hiding from my pain; it was to be found in my ability to confront my current situation and deal with it. So, I decided it was a good time to follow a new path that would lead me to my spiritual recovery as well. In order to continue to share in the joy of the Eucharistic Celebration I had reinstituted at my husband's funeral mass, Sunday Mass became a new staple in my life. While I prayed at home and at church, I asked for relief from the agony-laced heartache my grief had thrust upon me. I sought insight, a path to follow. Hopefully, I would be able to find a new purpose for my life.

Unfortunately, I also discovered going to church turned out to be emotionally difficult at times. I did my best to hold back my tears every time a thoughtful person approached me to offer their condolences. Just the mention of my husband's name was painful, but I forced myself to attend mass in spite of this fact. I enjoyed the spiritual enrichment my faith reinstated into my life, and I needed to face the difficult aspect of learning how to interact with people after the loss of my husband in order to overcome this adversity.

In the meantime, God provided many reasons for me to smile. Cookies, soup and even a cooked rack of lamb ended up at my doorstep at some of the lowest points in my recovery. Food was the last thing on my mind, but I always managed to nibble away at the thoughtful edibles that reached my table.

I'll never forget the kindness and compassionate acts of a dear friend who emailed me almost daily, to send a few words of encouragement, which made me feel as though she was thinking of me. It was nice to know people still cared!

Yet, as time slowly passed, I realized I had to address what proved to be a very difficult undertaking. My *third hurdle* tackled how I would become independent in my pursuits after the lifetime of joint ambitions my husband and I had lovingly shared.

When determining the direction our lives would take, the thoughts and dreams my husband and I had always pursued were always based upon a common denominator of two. Now that the equation had become a single integer of one, the million-dollar question was . . . how would I do this alone?

During the forty-nine years we spent together, our way of dealing with day to day issues was different than most. While we trusted our own judgement, we respected each other's opinion and enjoyed the process of decision making as a pair. Despite the fact that this worked out perfectly during our life-time together, after his death, it became an issue for me. For some unknown reason, I became riddled with guilt whenever I had to make a decision on my own. This may sound absurd since my husband was no longer alive, but suddenly, I felt as though I was making decisions behind my husband's back. It became another battle I needed to conquer.

So my challenge to deal with my phobia (that I was making wrong choices, or I was unable to make insignificant choices i.e. whether I should go shopping alone or call my sister to go with me) was solved when I finally asked myself, "What difference did it make, as long as I made a choice and moved on to the next obstacle?"

Then, my *fourth hurdle* was to create a new beginning in my life. It's not as though it was a novel idea, because it wasn't. But it was a good idea and an excellent place to start over. I made a list of everything I needed to address immediately, a to-do list which created structure in my life.

In the beginning, the list was simple: update my file at the Social Security Office, inscribe our names and pertinent information on our cemetery monument, and assemble the paperwork to probate my husband's estate.

Purposefully, I didn't make the list too long, for fear of being overwhelmed. Eventually, as the schedule grew shorter at the top end, I added to the bottom. There were so many things that needed to be done . . . all in good time!

When I crossed off an item on my agenda, the satisfaction I felt, at the accomplishment of the task, gave me strength to carry on. It also encouraged me to follow my quest to find the self-confidence I had lost at the time my husband died.

The *fifth and hardest hurdle* I faced dealt with ways to cope with the emptiness I felt as a result of my loss. My continuation of life was more difficult than I had ever imagined. The sounds of silence that echoed throughout the house, during the endless hours of each day, paled in comparison to my lonely nights. During the day, there were many occasions when I became overcome with grief without much provocation. At night, my anguish became insurmountable due to the absence of my husband's physical presence next to me. Each 24-hour cycle was a carousel ride of grief.

In response to my desperate prayers to God to help me accept His will, He heard and responded to my anguished pleas within a few days of my husband's passing. An unexpected spiritual experience occurred, which surprisingly gave me a purpose in life.

While asleep, with no one else in the house, I was awakened by the sound of my inner voice. It was a familiar voice, the same one I heard during hopeless situations in my past, when I had been unable to deal with other extreme difficulties my life's journey had placed before me.

The four distinct words which were spoken, *Alone in the darkness*, jolted me from my sound sleep. But, instead of helping me, the words confused me.

I was alone, yet the voice contradicted that fact . . . for now, I was no longer alone . . . I was with spirit. And so, this indescribable event comforted me, even though at the moment, I didn't understand its message. In reply, I thought, "I know I am alone in the darkness, but what do you mean?"

While I was excited and hoped to hear a response, when a reply wasn't forthcoming, in due course, I eventually fell back to sleep.

My explanation of this event began long ago . . . when I discovered I couldn't merely ask a question from my inner voice and expect to receive an answer on demand. My spirit doesn't speak to me by request. Instead, my inner voice will contact me when it feels the desperation of my situation and determines the level of my need.

The extraordinary spiritual communications I have been honored to receive usually result from a feeling of despondency I suffer at a particular moment in time.

There have been occasional instances when I have begged God to intercede in a special petition, and when His will didn't result in a response to my request, I would then ask Him to let me understand the reason for my distress, to help me endure the pain associated with the event.

I only hear from this subconscious inner voice when my spirit wants me to. In lieu of verbal responses, sometimes certain opportunities may be presented instead. There have only been a few occasions when I actually received a direct answer to a specific inquiry. These responses were short, yet the intent was profound.

Spiritual interactions are rare occurrences in my life. When God sends a messenger to answer my heartfelt prayers, I have faith the responses are an undeserved blessing. Most importantly, I am extremely grateful for God's gift, and I cherish His compassion in my time of need.

As the next day passed, and the shadowy darkness of the night hung over me, sleep again overcame my troubled mind. For the second night in a row, my inner voice spoke its intriguing message, *Alone in the darkness.*

No closer to understanding the reason for sending the words I clearly heard, once more I replied, "I do not understand." For the second night in a row, my earnest plea to grasp some idea of the spirit's meaning went unanswered . . . until sleep finally overcame me.

Following a third night of intense prayer, I again awoke to the words, *Alone in the darkness*. Only this time, I finally understood the meaning of the message, and I responded, "You want me to write a book."

After that night, I experienced spontaneous inspired writings which were so beautiful, I was compelled to write them down and incorporate them into my book. For many months thereafter, I continued to awake to creative thoughts weaving through my mind. Since I dare not chance the possibility of losing even a fragment of the intricate details disclosed to me, I forced myself to rise, seize the moment, and capture the precious thoughts, lest they be whisked away by forgetfulness brought upon me by my sleep. Yet, I needn't worry, for I knew sleep would elude me until I was totally satisfied I hadn't lost the important transcription of my dreams.

Finding a purpose, to help others cope and heal from the devastating ordeal of death became my quest . . . and it helped me heal!

I believe I had received the answer to my prayers. As my journey unfolded, soon a storyline of anguish began to appear on my white pages of hope, as my memoir soon became my therapy.

As I wrote each chapter, I cried, while I relived each heartfelt moment of sadness. Yet the mere thought of reassuring others . . . to understand, we can all make it through the darkest of times . . . was the message that drove me.

I felt inspired to explain the experiences my husband and I endured during our life, his death, and through my grief, as encouragement for other survivors to realize they won't suffer forever. Even if you don't believe in God or are angry at Him for your loss, He still hears your cries in the night during your anguish and pain. This is when He stands alongside of you, to support you . . . but you must understand, it is up to you to heed His message (of inspiration) and move on.

CHAPTER 35

My First Steps
Towards Independence

Even though I had finally found a purpose in my life, writing my book, I still had to deal with living my life, which was a completely different matter.

Because my mind continually dwelt upon my loss, and I couldn't concentrate on anything else, happiness eluded me. I faithfully cared for the dogs, as well as for myself, but little else interested me.

In spite of the fact that I went to church and occasionally to the grocery store with my sister and her husband, I had no desire to be sociable. It was too difficult to carry on a conversation without crying. I didn't want to put on airs that everything was okay, when it wasn't.

To make matters worse, I found decision making was a chore, and I wasn't up to the challenge. My brain was in a fog all the time, and I constantly worried I might have forgotten to attend to some important matter, which made me anxious.

The utilization of my new prioritized to-do list helped relieve some of my concerns because I finally had a reference point to determine what was crucial and what was not. As long as I wrote down the important matters which needed attention, I didn't have to stress over the little things which could be addressed at any time.

In addition to the Social Security change, the monument inscriptions, and the probate work, there was an important credit card classification I became aware of when I called to notify my credit card companies of my husband's death. Representatives from both a gas/fuel company and a department store informed me my account would be closed unless I applied for credit in my own name. Apparently, I was only an authorized user on the account and not a cardholder. Since I didn't use these accounts, I opted to close them instead.

Little bothersome details, like this, popped-up every so often. Although they weren't life shattering, they were still annoying.

The probating of an estate can be a monumental task. My experience as a legal secretary, when I handled probate matters in my younger years, enabled me to tackle this job on my own. While some estates don't require probating at all, for those that do, many survivors need help, which is available through the probate court or through an attorney. There are time constraints involved, with filing date requirements that must be met, so it is important to seek advice sooner rather than later when it comes to this issue.

Getting back to dealing with living my life, my sister knew I didn't like going to any store and preferred staying home instead. The few attempts I made to go with them didn't work out too well.

My husband and I always went everywhere together. While we shopped, if my husband was in a different part of the store, and I ran into friends or acquaintances, the first question I would always be asked was, "Where is your other half?"

Everyone who knew us took for granted, the fact that if I was present, my husband was nearby. While our personalities were like night and day, our relationship represented the yin-yang philosophy in the universe. We were split-a-parts who complemented each other.

After his death, these chance meetings were too upsetting. I had a hard-enough time answering the question, "How are you doing?" I certainly didn't want to meet people who weren't aware my husband had died, and then have to explain the sorrowful details. As a result of the negative effects I faced under these circumstances, until I could get my emotions under control, I chose to stay home and avoid the pain.

My sister and her husband were wonderful. They called all the time for grocery and pet supply lists, which she and her husband caringly delivered to my door. Thank goodness for their kindness or the dogs might have starved!

Common sense told me that I needed to move on, but this was much easier said than done. Then, out of the blue, inspiration struck again, as though fate had reached out to me. In addition to my current to-do list, I decided to create a bucket list of activities I thought might be enjoyable challenges.

While this idea wasn't an original one either, at least I was headed in the right direction. After I had jotted down a few items on my new list, one subject in particular stood out.

During my early grieving period, I only felt happy when I wrote. For that reason, I contemplated taking a college writing course to refresh my skills. When I was younger, I thought of dabbling in writing as a hobby, but time constraints never permitted trying my hand at this type of creativity. Since I now had nothing but time on my hands, I thought, what better chance would there be to seize the opportunity? What's more, if I took the course, I believed it would help polish my writing skills and possibly determine whether, or not, I had the ability to meet the expectations of a professor.

Now that the seed had been planted, I spent a great deal of time researching local colleges, their enrollment requirements, and the individual course syllabuses each university offered. Since the fall semester had already begun, my quest became an on-again, off-again search to determine which local college offered the most stimulating course available that met my criteria.

Although the idea sparked my fancy, I was uncertain if my emotions were under enough control to inspire me to register. The anticipation of attending school created a multitude of concerns, which I worried might create other barriers for me to overcome. There was plenty of time to decide, so I put the idea on the back burner and figured I would make up my mind at a later date.

Finally, I was looking ahead in my life, instead of in the rearview mirror, at a life which no longer existed.

When a luncheon invitation was extended to join family and friends at a local restaurant, I found myself hesitant to accept. Everyone thought it would be a great idea for me to get out of the house. Personally, I wasn't so sure.

To be honest, I really didn't want to go because I thought I might feel out of place . . . a third wheel. With that notion in mind, against my better judgement, I accepted.

It was strange how uncomfortable I felt at the thought of eating out with others. The security I enjoyed at home was unmistakable. Although it might be good for me to venture out, I worried if I would be able to portray any resemblance of strength during lunch, without falling apart. Despite the fact that I exhibited self-confidence on the outside, or so I had been told, I knew how fragile I still felt inside.

Prior to the luncheon date, during a few insecure moments, I considered calling my sister to cancel, but instead, I found the nerve to actually bite the bullet and make the best of it.

There was no doubt that I understood the importance of stepping out of my comfort zone. If I was to heal, I must rejoin society on my own, without my husband by my side. I could only hope that if I stayed focused on the positives and didn't think about the negatives while we were at lunch, I should be okay.

Of course, when the day finally arrived, there were some tears I successfully choked back during parts of our luncheon conversations. Then again, I discovered it was during these difficult moments, when I was at a loss for words, that I would be graciously carried along by my family and friends who were present.

My social luncheon gave me a platform to build upon, once I realized I actually had a good time. At this point, my newly gained confidence inspired me to take another leap of faith in my ability to move on.

My successful luncheon proved to me that the time had come for me to spread my wings a little. Because I had finally built up some self-reliance, I planned an unaccompanied trip to the mall to buy some jeans. After all, I was the new groundskeeper at my house and needed to dress the part.

This trip would be the first of many new beginnings, and I began to believe that my life was essentially headed in the right direction.

Considering the fact that decisive steps had been taken towards my own independence, it felt good to regain some of the self-determination I had lost at the time of my husband's death. In my mind's eye, although it was an uphill battle, I had indeed started my road to recovery.

CHAPTER 36

Communication from the Other Side

To my amazement, following his death, I believe my husband's spirit communicated with me by virtue of a multitude of otherworldly activities. It is my opinion that his spirit was just as upset as I was due to the separation his passing caused in our earthly relationship. Or else, the barrage of paranormal activities I encountered were meant to help me deal with my loss. Either way, he somehow managed to break the barriers between his world and mine, which convinced me that his essence lived on, and his soul had reached a new realm in which his life force now existed.

I am under the impression my husband's spirit made a conscientious effort to create detectable everyday events for me to experience, which might normally be associated with spiritual activity when they occur at exaggerated levels . . . instead of being considered a coincidence, when the incident only occurs once in a great while. For example, let's take a look at the light bulb scenario. One bulb blowing every month or so is a coincidence. On the other hand, because I had light bulbs blowing out all over the house, as well as in all of the garages, and the bulbs in the fixtures were flashing on and off without human intervention, in my opinion, these frequent unexplained phenomena suggested spiritual activity. For this reason, I believe these activities were orchestrated by my husband's spirit in order to encourage me to have faith that they represented proof of his spiritual presence in my life.

In view of the nature of these anomalies, it is hard to convince people who have never experienced spiritual or supernatural events, that these events are real. For some of us, these irregularities in nature really do exist. It might be sensible for a non-believer to say that certain deeds, such as lights flickering, light bulbs blowing, computer interference, or other similar anomalies are just a coincidence, but the manifestation of orbs, visions or apparitions can't be so easily explained.

Shortly after my husband's death, my sister and I speculated that my husband's spirit became very proficient at originating many of the incidents we witnessed at our respective homes. On numerous occasions, my sister would call to tell me the lights were flashing in her house, and as soon as I answered the phone and we spoke, my under counter lights would begin flickering as well.

The two of us became like little children, who were delighted in these new experiences, because we both believed all the paranormal abnormalities were directly connected to my husband's desire to communicate with us. Besides, these uncanny incidents were not limited to our two homes. My daughter also told us about incidents that occurred on separate occasions at her house, shortly after her father's death, which involved her curio cabinet lights and kitchen TV turning on by themselves. On another occasion, while I prepared to leave my house, the recessed hallway lights and the light fixture over the dinette table flickered at the same time. Whenever the lights would play this silly game, I stopped and waited until the activity ended, because I was intoxicated by the thought that my husband's spirit was with me at that moment. Often, I wondered how much energy his soul had to exert in order to be able to contact all of us in such diverse ways.

Most of the events which took place weren't scary. On the contrary, I was convinced they represented the manner in which a spirit reached out to the living once they transitioned over to their new dominion. From my experience, our spirit is a form of energy, which makes the execution of these activities seem more feasible.

For a short while after my husband's death, light bulbs continued to blow. When the frequency of the blowouts became an issue, especially due to the difficulty of replacing them in high ceiling locations in his work garage, I finally asked his spirit to please find another way to communicate with me.

The cessation of this particular activity took place immediately and was promptly replaced by a new accomplishment. Suddenly, his spirit learned how to access my computer because irregularities began to surface during my computer sessions. Despite the fact my husband wasn't totally proficient with computers during his lifetime, he discovered a way to take control over my laptop after his death.

The abnormalities started innocently enough one day, while I scrolled through my emails and my electronic messages began to roll non-stop. No matter what I did to retake control, I couldn't make the activity stop. Although this anomaly occurred on numerous occasions, during two separate instances, once the scrolling had ceased of its own accord, I determined it wasn't the message, it was the date on both emails that was significant, because both independent emails matched the date on which my husband had died.

Another heart-lifting event occurred one evening, as a result of painful memories I recalled while working into the night writing my story. When my tears began to gently roll down my face, I bowed my head in despair and darkness engulfed the room as my computer screen went blank. Although I realized it was my lack of productivity that had prompted the computer into its sleep mode, soon an unexpected light suddenly brightened the darkness around me. Inquisitively, I raised my head out of my hands and with teary eyes, I gazed upon the lightened screen to behold a picture of my husband with a slight smile upon his face.

There was no logical explanation to justify this feat. Even if some type of movement might have activated a reawaking of the computer screen, the folder where his photo was stored needed specific access for his picture to have appeared.

Though I truly believe my husband came to comfort me in a compassionate way, sometimes our acceptance of such mysterious events requires faith, in order to enjoy the solace our universe may unpredictably bestow upon us.

CHAPTER 37

Dreams

The meaning of the word dreams can be interpreted in many ways. As I have aged, I have learned that people look at life through various perspectives. So, when we begin to recognize there are basic differences between how people live their lives, it is usually dependent upon their own aspirations and the implementation of what it takes to make them happy. Therefore, when I speak of dreams, although my husband and I enjoyed a wonderful life together, our ambitions varied greatly. Despite this difference, we arrived at a similar destination, which was beneficial to us both. So, philosophically speaking, I thought it best to introduce my account of how dreams can influence our lives.

When I speak of my husband as a dreamer, I fondly remember the handsome young man, of meager means, with whom I fell in love. His dreams and ambitions soared above the clouds, and beyond the reach of what I thought would be humanly possible to achieve during our lifetime together. If I define the word dreamer in this context, I propose it to be the act of a person looking forward in life, towards a promising future.

Yet, when I speak of myself as a dreamer, another suggestion for the word's significance comes to mind. Despite the fact that I supported my husband in his earthly ambitions by every means possible, my dreams didn't consist of worldly gains. I found contentment and happiness in the love which surrounded me. And so, when I call myself a dreamer, I refer to the thoughts which enter my mind in the night, that sometimes serve as a parable for me to comprehend certain aspects of my life.

Personally, I feel the differences between these two explanations are simple to describe. My husband's dreams dealt with his worldly aspirations, which he so caringly conquered to support our lifetime together. While I, on the other hand, believed prayer was the answer to obstacles placed in our way, as we traveled through life together. So, instead of aspiring to conquer the world, I would pray, and sometimes dreams came to me in the night, which provided direction, intuition or the comforting insight I desired to solve the disturbing anxieties which troubled me.

To put it simply, my husband dreamed the dreams of the world, while I dreamed the dreams of the spirit.

Within a few weeks after my husband's death, I had a very vivid dream. As I lay alone in bed, I felt the presence of a person standing next to me. I envisioned a man dressed in black with a crisp crease down the front of his pants, and the shininess of the buckle on his black belt created a lasting image in my mind. My belief, that the person who stood next to me was a priest, was overpowering. This sensation was embellished by the fact that I was fascinated by a vague perception that I could actually hear him breathing.

As soon as I reached the point where I visualized a black leather prayer book in his hands, instinctively, I was convinced the priest was there to administer the Sacrament of the Last Rites, or the Blessing of the Sick as it is now called. I didn't open my eyes to look because I didn't want this personification to end.

Unafraid, I spiritually pondered if I, too, would die shortly? Might my dream possibly be an omen of my future, or lack thereof?

At that moment, I thought of the many times in the last few months when my husband told me he was ready to die; yet I often wondered, if he was afraid of death.

I was amazed when I felt calm and undaunted at the thought of my own demise. I remember thinking . . . I am at peace and ready to accept whatever path God has chosen for me; when suddenly, the dream ended, and I opened my eyes.

Now, I felt comfort in the belief my dream was God's way of letting me know my husband's death was a peaceful one. I was grateful to God for the insight of this possibility, and I thanked Him for His compassion in providing me a plausible answer to my concern.

Although my life hasn't been full of prophetic dreams which have controlled my destiny, in some instances, my dreams have been helpful in providing simple solutions, when ordinary resolutions lay just beyond my reach.

It is reasonable to say, my existence has been profoundly enriched by my enchanting dreams because they have presented me with thought-provoking philosophies, which have contributed to who I am.

CHAPTER 38

I Didn't Look Forward to The Start of the Holidays

Time seemed to pass uneventfully once I became engaged in my writing, until suddenly, the holiday season was upon me. While the days inched closer to Thanksgiving, I found no joy in the anticipation of this year's upcoming celebration.

Due to the loss of my husband's parents and the aging of mine, our family holiday responsibilities were altered a long time ago when my husband and I took over the duties of hosting our traditional Thanksgiving dinner. As the years marched on, my father died, and attendees dwindled, yet, we still carried on the holiday custom because we both believed it was important to share this special family activity together.

My outlook on life changed after my husband died, and I wondered if I would be able to carry on the holiday tradition . . . or, if I even wanted to.

So, I asked my sister what she thought I should do regarding my indecisiveness about hosting Thanksgiving dinner this year. She understood how difficult it would be for me to endure this first major holiday without my husband. Therefore, she sympathetically encouraged me to decide what was best for me.

"I support any decision you make, and everyone will make due accordingly," was her compassionate reply.

Inspired by her empathy, I no longer felt obligated to make an immediate decision, which gave me time to consider my current situation. Even though our family gathering would be small, and dinner would only include the five of us, I was sad when I visualized our family dinner without my husband sitting at the head of the table, cracking jokes and providing the helping hand he always contributed to my enjoyment of the day.

Undeniably, I wasn't in a celebratory mood, but I also knew my decision would be instrumental in our family's enjoyment of the upcoming holiday season. Since Thanksgiving represented a time of year when we expressed our thanks for the blessings bestowed upon us, I thought, what better way could there be to fortify our family unity than to get together for an enjoyable meal? After all, no matter how severely my husband's loss affected us all, we still had so much to be thankful for.

Since I couldn't find fault with my reasoning, I accepted the fact that life must go on and decided family harmony would be my fundamental motivation to carry on our traditional Thanksgiving celebration.

Therefore, in preparation for our holiday meal, I purchased a fresh turkey for our entrée while the rest of my family planned to bring various side dishes to supplement our tiny feast.

When Thanksgiving morning arrived, I rose early, as usual, in order to prepare the bread stuffing my mother-in-law had taught me to make so many years ago, since this was my daughter's favorite side dish at Thanksgiving. While sautéing the onions in butter, which would be mixed with the shredded fresh bread I had prepared the night before, I felt lonely without my husband's company. I missed the sound of his voice, his quirky humor, as well as the helping hand he was always so eager to provide. The emptiness of our house seemed worse than normal. To combat my loneliness, I had turned on the TV to keep me company, while I worked in the kitchen alone.

Once the turkey was stuffed and properly basted, I placed it in the oven. It was still early, for I had allowed plenty of cooking time for our scheduled noontime celebration, and it was now time for me to focus on the rest of my cooking chores. After I washed the dishes and cleared my workspace, I turned my attention to peeling the potatoes for the mashed potatoes and gravy we all would enjoy. The fresh New England clam chowder I had prepared the day before still needed to be heated, but there was plenty of time for that once my company arrived.

I still planned to prepare an hors d'oeuvre of some fresh shrimp, to be chilled and served with a side dish of cocktail sauce. Chips with dip, plus pickles and olives would complete my list of appetizers. Once I made the gravy, and the turkey reached it peaked juicy tenderness with crispy brown skin, my cooking responsibilities would be done.

My sister had taken on the chore of preparing a family size serving of sautéed mushrooms, plus a large bowl of fresh organic coleslaw, while my daughter and son-in-law would enhance our array of appetizers with a tray of deviled eggs. Predictably, once everyone made their contributions and the celebration began, there would be way too much food for the five of us to eat, but, that was our tradition at Thanksgiving.

By now, the stuffed turkey had been baking in the oven for hours, with its delicious aroma permeating throughout the house. In order to complete my hostess duties, the time had come to take out the holiday china and arrange the place settings for our upcoming meal.

Unprepared for the emotions which swept over me, unanticipated tears began to roll down my cheeks when I walked into the dining room and looked at the empty table and chairs. How could such a normal everyday activity like setting a table cause me such pain? This led me to wonder if it would be less traumatic for me if we all ate in the kitchen instead? Why was it so hard for me to decide?

Suddenly, I realized it was the unexpected loss I felt when I looked at my husband's empty chair that had saddened me. Unwilling to deal with my emotions, I turned and left the room.

In need of a resolution for the unforeseen predicament I now faced, I knew I had a difficult decision to make. Although the question, "Where would I set the table for us to eat" was simple, I was emotionally unable to provide a suitable answer.

To appease my anguish, I was in desperate need of a distraction. When I reached the kitchen, I switched the TV channels in search of a happier show to watch, which enabled me to establish a better frame of mind. I also began to think of happier days, when our Thanksgiving table was filled with loving family members, and those fond memories brightened my hopes of finding some holiday cheer.

Shortly thereafter, the doorbell rang. When I opened the door, I was met by smiling faces. As my daughter, sister and their husbands entered the house, with their arms full of tasty items to make our dinner complete, they expressed a host of warm, welcoming greetings.

Once everyone settled in, the munching began. As wine was poured into long-stemmed glasses, happy chatter filled the room, and the aroma of the slow-cooking turkey enticed us all.

Before long, activities were underway in preparation for the celebration of our Thanksgiving meal, at which time my daughter casually peeked into the dining room. In an inquisitive tone, she asked, "Mom, why haven't you set the table yet?"

I had hoped to pass on this painful decision without making a big deal out of my dismay, so I replied to her question with one of my own, "Do we want to continue eating in the dining room, like usual, or start a new tradition and eat in the kitchen instead?"

"What's wrong with where we usually eat?" was my daughter's response.

I was unable to reply. With my guard down, I began to choke back my tears, because the decision involved an emotional issue and wasn't a matter of logistics.

Due to my distress, an awkwardness enveloped the room. So, my family threw the ball back into my court by kindheartedly offering to let me decide.

"Maybe I shouldn't have had Thanksgiving after all," was my initial thought, but I quickly eliminated that idea from my mind. Suddenly, the choice was no longer a difficult one to make, because I wasn't alone any more, my family was by my side.

My decision now became clear, and I replied with a smile, "We will continue our tradition. We will eat in the dining room."

While she gathered the plates, I asked my daughter to include a setting for her Dad as well, and a huge smile accompanied her nod of agreement.

Once the savory turkey was cooked and placed on the counter ready to be served, my son-in-law took over the paring duties. While he expertly carved the turkey, we arranged the table with the rest of the food, in anticipation of our approaching meal.

Soon, our plates were piled high with roasted turkey and stuffing, as we all gathered around the table to share in our blessings. Before we ate, we prayed and thanked God for the graces He bestowed upon us.

We all laughed a little, and cried a little. Although my husband wasn't with us physically, his spirit was present in all our hearts. He was an integral part of our celebration, in our toast salutations and in our shared memories of the past.

Though initially uncertain I would enjoy hosting Thanksgiving this year, it turned out that I found comfort in our family unity which, unquestionably, was the main reason for our gathering. Although the day had included some sadness, as well as joy, there was no doubt I had made the right choice. The holiday was definitely worth celebrating, and our tradition would carry on!

CHAPTER 39

An Essence of Peace

I t was Monday, the 7th of December, Pearl Harbor Day, and my chores for the day included going to the post office, the bank and the store to purchase some dog food.

Due to the significance of this day in American History and my tremendous esteem for military veterans, especially my husband, I suddenly felt a strong desire to drive to the cemetery to spend a few moments at my husband's gravesite.

Even though I was headed in the opposite direction, I knew this yearning needed to be satisfied, or else I would deal with regret for the rest of the day. So, I turned around to show my respect at the graveyard.

During my drive, I looked forward to the tranquility I hoped my visit would provide, even though I knew a grave was just the resting place for our bodily remains, and my husband's spirit was now free of its earthly constraints.

After I parked the car and approached the familiar granite marker, a smile slowly emerged upon my face.

When I gazed across the graveyard, I found myself alone, except for the silhouette of a lone older woman heading in my direction. It was then, I imagined what her thoughts might be as she walked along past me with a look of contentment upon her face. She gave me the impression she was at peace, and I silently wondered if she was visiting her long-lost love's resting place to find solace, like me.

Once the woman had disappeared from view, sadness overtook me when I thought about how difficult it was to overcome the absence of a loved one. It was then, that I placed my hands upon our headstone and wished my loving thoughts would reach my husband's soul.

Although the air was warm, the stone was cold, and instead of receiving the comforting relief I desired, I perceived a chilly sense of death, which merely served to reaffirm the sad reality that he had died.

There was no doubt, I still needed time to overcome the absence of my husband's presence in my life. So, while slowly walking away, with my heart full of love, I wondered just how long it would take before I could be the charming lady who strolled along emitting an essence of peace.

CHAPTER 40

Temptation

During my drive home, after my visit to the cemetery and the completion of my scheduled tasks, my concentration was distant. I felt as though I was lost in a fog, moving along on autopilot. When I reached my driveway, stopping to pick up my mail revitalized my thoughts from my somber frame of mind.

The evergreen trees we had planted many years ago displayed the only array of green amidst the acres of leafless oak trees. The sounds of birds chirping, as they nestled in the trees, brightened my dreary midwinter outlook, since their singing reminded me of nature's transformation which would take place in early spring.

Once back in my car, I continued down the driveway and heard an excited commotion. It was my dogs, who always left the warmth of their cozy outside beds behind to eagerly greet me at the chain-link fence when I returned.

At the moment, though pleased by their attention, I could only verbally respond to their presence. Speaking as though they should understand my salutation, I smiled and said, "Hi guys." My welcoming gesture would have to suffice until I got inside and brought them in to join me for a proper greeting.

It was late afternoon, when I pulled into the garage, and the sun was already setting. With the car's transmission now in park, I reached up and pressed the button to close the garage door behind me. Suddenly I was oblivious of my surroundings. A state of confusion and bewilderment had unexpectedly overpowered me, as I sat behind the wheel. In slow motion, I turned and looked toward the door, which led into the house. But the fact that I should turn off the car, collect my packages and go inside was now beyond my comprehension.

While sitting motionlessly, in a trance, and staring straight ahead, mindless of my current situation, a mysterious, pleasant feeling of calmness overwhelmed me. It was a Utopian experience, and momentarily, I was in awe of my serenity.

Then, out of nowhere, a deep, low, quiet, and compelling voice gave me a message, while the car continued to run. I was mesmerized as the voice enticed me to close my eyes, relax, go to sleep and leave my worries behind. The idea was almost impossible to refute, for the soothing encouragement of the voice sounded so inviting.

Spellbound, I found myself frozen in time, unable to move, while I barely heard the background noise of the engine humming. However, somehow I knew, I understood that this voice wasn't my spirit's voice, the one I identified with good.

Although totally unaware of the danger I was in, suddenly I shook my head, as though a mental jolt released me from my enchantment. I promptly regained control of my senses and shut off the car, which abruptly ended the threatening situation.

I was convinced a malicious entity had enticed me, in a most cunning and decisive way, by luring me into a disturbing experience which could easily have taken my life that day.

Unquestionably, the message conveyed was of serenity, and not of grief, or despair, because whatever had grabbed hold of my free will understood, I wouldn't respond to giving up hope in my life, so it chose to use tranquility and peacefulness as its bait instead.

Could a negative energy have tried to stop me from helping others deal with their anguish and sorrow? Had some ominous entity tried to prevent my encouraging words from being heard through my story?

The answer to this mystery is something I will never know for sure, but I believe God watches over us, and He was well aware of my struggle.

The release of the power which controlled me felt as though I had been awakened from a dream, because I was amazed by the internal burst of energy I experienced when its influence was broken.

Unquestionably, I believe a spiritual intervention had allowed *me* to decide my fate that day.

I trust that God offers each one of us guidance and aims to shelter us against the evils of the world. Though, in order to benefit from His blessings, we in turn must honor, have faith, and be devout in our love for Him.

Just like the spectrum of a rainbow produces the beautiful array of colors we enjoy as the droplets of water descend from the sky, the abundance of intuition we receive from God are like droplets of knowledge to help properly guide us through our lives.

Comparatively speaking, there are portions of a rainbow we may not always see, which can be obscured by the clouds in the sky, yet the rainbow in its entirety still exists.

Likewise, God's love is infinite, but our ability to benefit from His benevolence may be dependent upon the degree of faith we behold in Him.

CHAPTER 41

A Hallmark Card

I t was Christmas Eve day, and almost two and a half months had passed since my husband's death. While working on my book in my home office, I happened to look out the window. Through the bare oak trees, I saw a lone automobile traveling down the driveway. Since I wasn't expecting company and didn't recognize the vehicle, I watched as the truck pulled into the turn-around area and parked.

Once the driver emerged from behind the wheel and started heading towards my door, I immediately recognized the man to be a former business associate, whom my husband and I had met a long time ago. Throughout the years, we had become good friends.

As he approached the house, I opened the office door to invite him in, since it was nice to see a friendly face during my self-imposed seclusion.

With a card in hand, he told me how truly sorry he was for my loss. Like so many people in this day and age, he didn't subscribe to any of the local newspapers, therefore he had just heard about my husband's death the week before.

While expressing his sorrow, I became aware that a tear had formed in his eye. When he said, "I didn't think it was enough to just mail a card, so I came to express my sympathy in person," the true depth of his compassion became clear.

Touched by the fact that he had taken time out of his busy schedule to stop by and personally convey his comforting remarks, I assumed he had searched far and wide for the special Hallmark Card which proclaimed, "Your Husband Was a Good Man." Unquestionably, I couldn't have agreed more with this assertion.

Although the visit was short, his compassion was genuine and reassuring, and I held his sympathy in high esteem. It is important to note that a survivor derives substantial benefit from fond memories, or condolences for their loved ones who have died. That is why I believe it is never too late to convey consoling thoughts.

CHAPTER 42

Harmony

The holiday season was in full swing, and continuously revived melancholy thoughts of vivid memories of my past. Obviously, this wouldn't be my first Christmas alone, without my husband to share in the holiday cheer, because during our budding relationship while he served in Vietnam, we were an ocean apart. And since we all have to play the hands we are dealt, my objective was to figure out a way to make this holiday bearable.

Christmas had always been a favorite time of year for me because my loving memoirs bring back one of my life's happiest moments. Vividly, I remember Christmas from almost half-a-century ago, when at the end of the day and while alone in his car, my husband shaped a tender memory I will never forget. He had waited until after all the holiday gifts were opened, and the official gift giving part of Christmas had passed, before he placed an engagement ring upon my finger. He said the ring wasn't a gift, it was a promise, which represented a pledge of our love and the future we would share together.

While Thanksgiving with my family went better than I had expected, the thought of experiencing my first Christmas alone was discouraging.

Obviously, under the circumstances, my previous Christmas expectations of sharing our pledge of love would never be the same. So instead, I needed to seek contentment in my life by searching for joy in the simplicity of the meaning of Christmas.

Fortunately, my daughter and her husband were content to spend a quiet day resting at home during this Christmas season. Therefore, my sister and I chose to spend time together with our aging mother, who lived in a nearby nursing home.

The decision was unanimous. Christmas would be simple, a small team effort between my sister, her husband and me, to help me regain some Christmas spirit, in an amicable effort to find Peace on Earth and Goodwill To All Men.

With the arrival of Christmas, my sister and her husband supported me by attending early morning services at my Church. The sanctuary, adorned with impressive red and white poinsettias, nestled near lush evergreens with red ribbons cascading down their sides, was beautiful. Every holiday shrub was decorated with small, white twinkling lights. The altar positively glowed with nature's beauty!

The beautiful ornamentation displayed this time of year put a smile on my face, as I envisioned my husband, in his youth, being inspired by similar sights. I pictured him as a young boy, with a grin on his face, in anticipation of the presents he hoped to receive. I enjoyed the thought of the delight such images would bestow upon him as a child.

Following our spiritual cerebration, we emerged to warm, gentle breezes, which softly caressed our faces. Bright sunshine had replaced the early morning fog of a comfortable December morning. While standing outside, mingling with friends, absorbing the warm rays of the sun, I imagined that if the day had been an earlier time in my life and my husband was present, my morning would have been perfect. Instead, my spirits were suddenly dampened when the sorrowful thought of my loss crept back into my mind, as it often did without warning.

During our short drive to the cemetery, as the sun shined into the car, I presumed our ability to find happiness over time is dependent upon our acceptance of changes in our life, that we simply must learn to endure.

While standing by our headstone, thinking of the wonderful memories my husband and I had shared, I spent a private moment of reflection. Because I had allocated a portion of my Christmas celebration to spend time with the memory of my husband, I benefited emotionally from this meditation, and my frame of mind improved.

By now it was late morning, and we set off to enjoy our scheduled Christmas breakfast before we embarked upon our visit to our mother, to spread some holiday cheer.

Mom's space was bright and sunny, and she enjoyed the extra warmth the southern exposure delivered into her room. Although she no longer remembered our names, she quickly recognized our friendly faces. We could tell she was happy to see us by the joy that gleamed in her eyes and the smile that radiated upon her face. This reaction was always followed by an affectionate kiss that she would present each one of us upon our arrival. Though young at heart, at 96, she had already lost a good portion of her hearing, and it was too difficult to carry on a conversation. So, instead, we kept her company and watched cheerful Christmas shows on TV until her special Christmas meal was served, which meant it was time for us to go.

As it turned out, the harmony our small family gathering delivered on Christmas Day helped me fill the void that loneliness had torn into my broken heart. There were no lavish gifts, just precious time we shared together. My desire to give comfort, to bestow the peace on earth I sought, is what got me through the day.

Our small Christmas celebration had opened my eyes to see that I could find happiness through compassion for our mother, even during my own difficult time of need.

CHAPTER 43

I Walked My Way Through Darkness, Toward the Light

My sister and her husband had been kind enough to plan the celebration of their Christmas around me. So, when it was time to go home after the visit with our mother, I settled into the back seat of their car with a surprised feeling of contentment. Because the day's activities were so private during our intimate little settings at the restaurant and the nursing home, I didn't feel as though I had celebrated a major Christmas event, just a quiet cozy one. It was the most enjoyable way I could have spent the day, and I was grateful to them both for their thoughtfulness.

When my brother-in-law drove along the familiar roads I had always driven while my husband was still alive, I unexpectedly found myself lost in a daydream. I was back in time, driving home from visiting my mother, anticipating my husband sitting on our front porch awaiting my return.

The realistic image caused me to break down in tears when I suddenly realized my true world did not include such happiness.

Though I tried to hide my anguish, the muffled sounds of my sobbing became noticeable over the soft music playing on the CD in the car.

Now aware of my grief, my sister didn't understand the cause of my distress until I explained my vision and its unintended affect upon my happiness.

My heartache was insurmountable, and no matter how hard she tried, my sister couldn't calm my outburst of tears. Upon reaching home a short while later, I declined their kind offer to come in to comfort me. All I wanted was to be left alone.

My emotional outburst was an issue I needed to deal with on my own. Sadness was my response to the tricks my mind played, in its attempts to deny my husband's death.

Now that I was home alone, I needed to find a way to combat my distress. There was still sunlight left to the day, and the warmth from the afternoon sun afforded me the opportunity to do some work outside, even though it was Christmas. Since I wasn't sure how much longer the warmer temperatures would last, and I needed to concentrate on a specific project in order to get into a better frame of mind, I decided to wash my car.

Once I started the job, I did feel better. While I worked, I reminisced about the many times I would look over to see my husband cleaning our vehicles, as I worked on other outside chores. It was a happy memory, which enhanced the satisfaction I felt upon completion of the job.

While I began to put everything neatly away, dusk slowly overtook the remaining sunlight of Christmas Day. It surprised me to realize that my gloomy mood had improved. I had found satisfaction in my ability to win my battle to overcome my grief, because I had managed to turn a distressing situation around through my positive actions.

The distractions I created, in order to endure the circumstances which caused me pain, became instrumental in my recovery. Although my mind wasn't functioning properly during my early grief, which made it difficult to think of alternative actions; over time, a positive behavioral response to negativity became second nature to me.

Since Christmas was now officially over, and soon a new year would begin, my emotional mountains and valleys were becoming a bit more manageable. It felt good to have the hardest part of the holiday season behind me. I intended to continue to do my best to put one foot in front of the other, and walk my way through darkness toward the light.

CHAPTER 44

Remembrance

On Friday, the 8th of January, I was surprised to receive a call from a nurse's aide, who worked in the Oncology Department at the Providence VA. She told me that the VA Medical Center Chaplain Service was preparing a special Interfaith Service of Remembrance to honor those veterans who were transferred into Palliative Care and had died during the last quarter of 2015 as a result of their service to our Country. The ceremony would be held on January 28, 2016, on the 3rd floor Chapel of the Providence VA Medical Center.

During our conversation, it took a minute before I understood what the call was all about. I suddenly experienced an agonizing, reawaking of my grief as I wrote down the information detailing the time, place and location of the service.

"There is no question, I will be there" was my heartfelt response.

Even though the service would be small, the woman assured me the commemorative ceremony was very well organized. Believing I would find comfort by attending, she suggested that many of the previous relatives, who attended similar services in the past, were grateful for the hard work the Chaplin and other hosts had contributed to assembling this memorial event.

Following the call, a flood of tears overcame me. Though I welcomed the opportunity to attend, my slowly recovering heart suddenly felt as though it had been ripped open, and I would be attending my husband's funeral all over again.

Since I had been told that I was allowed to bring family members to participate in the service, I invited my sister and her husband to join me. As usual, they were more than willing to offer their support. Had they declined, it would have been quite an excursion to tackle on my own. Nevertheless, no matter how difficult the trip might have been, I would have gone alone if I had to.

The next three weeks passed quickly, and the morning of the service had arrived. Fortunately, the weather continued its warming trend, so the roads were clear, and the drive was easy.

Upon our approach to the hospital, the memory of my husband walking alongside me the last time we were there was painful. It broke my heart to walk the same halls without him, because it conjured up the hopelessness we both felt on the last day we left the hospital together.

When we reached the cozy little chapel, we were greeted by the Chaplin. He was a very pleasant individual and offered us coffee, cookies and breakfast snacks, which had been laid out on a table at the rear of the chapel for those in attendance to enjoy.

Since we were the first family members to arrive, we entered into a friendly conversation with him. He explained that the ceremony was meant to provide an honorary tribute to those who had died, while at the same time, benefit the surviving family members as well. The service aimed to provide a form of closure some of the next of kin might still be pursuing for their loved ones who had died, especially for those families who may not have been able to afford a funeral.

Even though the chapel was small, it emanated a feeling of comfort and peace. The room's ambiance was similar to that of a small church, with approximately fifteen rows of pews lining the sides of a center aisle which led up to the alter. Sunlight streamed through the stained-glass windows onto the rose-colored, tile flooring. A brown baby grand piano stood to the left of the altar. It would be played in accompaniment of the services to be performed in the forthcoming ceremony. A beautiful quilted comforter, adorned with stars and stripes and two blue eagles, sat prominently at the end of the aisle, in front of the altar.

As family members arrived, everyone was instructed to write down the name of the deceased veteran they were there to honor on a chalkboard located outside the chapel door.

When the time came for the ceremony to begin, most of the pews were filled with solemn faces of relatives who wanted to participate in honoring the fallen soldiers who had died.

The service consisted of prayers, songs, and the reading of a grief poem entitled: *Should You Go First* by Albert Kennedy "Rosey" Rowsell. During the reading of this sad and touching poem, there wasn't a dry eye in the room. Toward the end of the ceremony, the Chaplin began calling the names of the deceased military soldiers who were being honored. I proudly walked up to the podium when my husband's name was called. A white carnation with an anonymous dog tag attached, plus a small, stamp-size memorial sticker flag was presented to me, as well as to each family member present, as a symbolic gesture of appreciation. The sticker flag was then placed by each recipient, upon a small service plaque which represented the branch of the military in which the soldier had served.

The heartfelt effort, respect, and sympathy, contributed by each member of the Chaplain's Service, inspired everyone present. In my opinion, their mission to provide consolation to the living by remembering their loved ones who had died, had been successfully accomplished.

CHAPTER 45

There is Life After Death –
I Have Seen and Felt Its Presence

My grief returned with a vengeance since the scheduling of the VA memorial ceremony. In view of the fact it had only been a mere four months since I became widowed, that wasn't nearly enough time for my heart to heal, much less, become accustomed to my loss when my husband's memory crossed my mind . . . which was often.

Just like the Monsignor had predicted, during my early grief, spiritual activities increased with the passage of time. For those who don't believe a spiritual realm exists outside of our own, these experiences are hard to describe. I find it difficult to explain how my mind can see objects, or visions, which logically should be invisible to the naked eye. With these thoughts in mind, I will delve into the spiritual experiences I have encountered, including some that have gone far beyond my own expectation of believability.

It was a dark, lonely, mid-January evening, and while relaxing in bed, watching a show to keep me company, I had fallen asleep with the TV still on. Afterwards, as often happens, I awoke to the sight of a dense fog in my bedroom, which merely intrigued me. Even though I still couldn't explain the fog's purpose, I was no longer afraid of its manifestation, so I watched until it vanished before my eyes in an uneventful manner.

Since I was accustomed to this abnormality, I wasn't fazed by the event. At the same time, I was tired, and it was time for peace and quiet, which hopefully would lead to an uninterrupted rest. Since the TV had become a distraction in my endeavor to fall back to sleep, I picked up the remote and pressed the button to shut it off. When the TV didn't turn off, I was annoyed with myself because I assumed I had hit the wrong function button. During my next attempt, to make sure I did it right, I raised my arm up and angled the remote in order to catch some rays of light from the lit TV screen. I soon discovered, after I purposefully aimed and hit the off button, the TV continued to play. After several more tries, I decided the time had come to test if I would be able to change the channels or adjust the voice control, but all of these attempts failed as well.

Frustrated, my thoughts turned to the only likely explanation I had left . . . my husband's spirit had something to do with this event.

Intent upon finding a resolution to my problem, I appealed to his spirit's kindness and said, "I'm glad you came to visit me, but I need some sleep." Hoping for positive results, I immediately gave the selector one last try. Although the voice and channel controls didn't respond, when I hit the off button, the TV turned off on my first try.

I smiled when I laid my head back down upon my pillow because I believed that I had regained control as a direct result of his assistance.

Expecting the rest of my night to be peaceful, I was surprised when a short while thereafter, I awoke to the sight of an object floating on the right side of my bed. It was greenish in color, about the size of an avocado, and looked like a small football with a tiny, intricate grid pattern resembling metal fencing. The object's appearance was fascinating and so beautiful, it reminded me of a delicately created piece of jewelry. I interpreted the oblong entity to be a type of orb, and I was unhappy when it floated through the closed window and disappeared from my view. Undaunted by this new experience, I fluffed my pillow and dozed off for the third time.

Then, a little after 2 AM, I was startled from my sleep when I felt something nudge me. Confused and somewhat alarmed by the sensation that I had been touched, I immediately sat up and searched my room for evidence of its cause. Although nothing seemed to be amiss, I was too shaken and alert to lay back down and try to sleep. Disturbing thoughts that my paranormal experiences might be elevating to a level of physical contact, unexpectedly became a daunting possibility.

Since it was the middle of the night and I needed to distract my fretful mind, I thought it best to turn on the TV until my unsettled nerves could quiet down. Recalling the unusual issues I had encountered earlier that night, I smiled when I picked up the remote, pressed the start button and it turned on. While trying to soothe my apprehension, a comforting thought crossed my mind. I fancied the possibility that my husband had meant to cheer me up after the resurgence of my grief, by playing this spirited prank on me. A calming serenity followed my cheerful thoughts of his imaginable new found remote control abilities, which finally enabled me to relax. No longer troubled by anxiety, I shut off the TV and fell into a deep sleep.

A few hours later, an unfamiliar bewildering encounter began. While laying on my side, with my head resting upon my pillow while I slept, I faced toward the triple window located on the right side of my bed. *Words cannot describe* exactly how I felt at the moment I realized there was an up and down movement of my mattress in the vicinity of my head. Although I was sound asleep a second ago, I suddenly found myself wide awake. Frightened, but not terrified, I wondered what type of spiritual activity could be causing this perplexing incident, but I was hesitant to open my eyes to see if a visible entity accompanied this unexplained event. Now I realized, though I was intimidated by this nerve-wracking experience, I must confront my fears. A few unsettling seconds passed before

I built up the courage to look and see what was causing the ongoing movement, since I knew there was no one else in the house but me.

When I opened my eyes and searched the space in front of me, there was no visible entity, and the movement stopped abruptly. Now, anxiously speculating about what would happen next, I laid perfectly still and listened as I stared into the darkness.

While silently hoping this experience had concluded, my anticipation of a termination of this scary scenario vanished when I began to feel a heaviness, a pressure on my husband's side of the bed, accompanied by creaking noises from the mattress. It sounded and felt as though a person sat down, laid down, and then turned over on their side, presumably in an attempt to get comfortable for a good night's rest.

Stricken with anxiety, I now wondered if my husband's spirit had gained a bizarre ability which allowed him to enter my earthly realm, but as much as I missed him, I was not joyfully anticipating an actual supernatural interaction.

It took tremendous courage to turn over, to look and see if an apparition accompanied this mystifying activity. When I stared into the hazy darkness on my husband's side of the bed, I was relieved when I determined that no physical man-ifestation accompanied this unnerving event, and the activity immediately ceased.

Granted, I should have been horrified by this alarming incident, but to my surprise, I was not. I believe that the many years of otherworldly experiences I have encountered are to thank for that. But, I remember wondering if this experience might possibly have been a dynamic attempt by his spirit to be close to me and comfort me? It was gratifying to believe he might have compassionately reached from his world into mine. This rationalization comforted me and eased my anxiety. Now that loving thoughts had replaced my fears, I relaxed and fell asleep for the remainder of the night.

Although the next evening was peaceful and uneventful, two nights thereafter, I awoke to the sight of a manifested embodiment of a human form, which had been watching me as I slept while it stood silently at the foot of my bed. Initially, I believed it was the spirit of my husband, and therefore I became captivated by its presence.

While I watched the eerie figure in amazement, the thought that someone might have broken into my home suddenly entered into my mind. I felt my heart race as I stared at the dark shadowy form which stood motionless in front of me, in the stillness of the night.

To ensure my safety against an intruder of the human kind, I quickly looked over at the alarm system's keypad to make sure I had turned it on. After confirming the system had been activated, I now believed for certain that it was my husband's spirit, because no one could have entered my house without triggering the alarm.

The unearthly apparition stood a little over 6 ft. tall, my husband's approximate height. It appeared to have the outline of a head, set on the shoulders of a body, with arms draping straight down alongside its indiscernible form. No neck was visible, nor were the arms distinguishable from the chest, although the rounded appearance of a person's upper shoulders was evident.

Despite the fact the supernatural figure looked humanlike, it had no obvious facial features or defining characteristics that I could describe. This time, instead of the smoky consistency which usually enveloped my room, the spirit's form was dark in color and solid looking, while the atmosphere around its presence was clear.

An average person might have been disturbed by the sight, but I was enchanted by its ghostly presence because I was confident the manifestation which stood before me was my husband's spirit. Given that the apparition exhibited no threatening gestures or harmful intent, in barely a whisper I said, "Hi, Sweetheart."

In response to my communication, in less than an instant, the figure started to float towards me from its previous stationary stance.

Not knowing what to expect next, I unexpectedly became frightened! Therefore, I closed my eyes for a moment, and when I opened them, the visitation had ended.

Originally, amazed by this awesome sight, I wanted it to last . . . until the prospect of the apparition approaching me had quickly changed my mind. Initially, I had been comforted by this unearthly presence, and I marveled at the powers of the universe which enabled me to see, what I believed to be, my husband's spirit. But I soon discovered, I wasn't strong enough to behold the face hiding in the shadows, as the manifestation quickly approached me.

The sight of a dark, otherworldly spirit moving in direct response to my verbal exchange, as though it had waited for my communication, suggested a spiritual interaction beyond my initial belief. Not only did life after death seem to be a certainty to me, but due to the other paranormal activities I recently experienced, I now believed that the love of the spirit continued on as well.

Since I was unable to comprehend the apparition's intent as it approached me, I became frightened and now thought that his essence belonged in another realm and not at the foot of my bed. Though the encounter was brief, undeniably, the veil between our two dimensions had been crossed.

Five days of tranquil nights elapsed since the last uncanny manifestation took place. I had just gotten accustomed to the serenity, when again, I was awakened by the same movement of my mattress. I could only assume my calm acceptance of the previous two events allowed my husband to believe I was okay with this type of visitation. Only now, the thought of this happening on a regular basis really scared me!

No matter how much I loved and missed my husband, I knew it was unnatural for this type of association to exist between a soul of the living and a spirit of the dead. I told him, "This isn't right, it cannot be." The movement stopped immediately and neither incident ever occurred again.

Before my husband's death, I never imagined experiencing the paranormal interactions which occurred. In retrospect, I often wondered if the spiked resurgence of my grief since the scheduling of the VA's Service of Remembrance Ceremony could have resulted in these spiritual visitations? Was it a coincidence, the first of the three encounters occurred two nights after I received the initial call on the 8th of January?

Of course, there is no way to be certain, but I do believe the visitations weren't meant to scare me. I have faith that they were intended to help me in my emotional time of need.

Additionally, there were other similar incidents which occurred almost two years after my husband's death. I had been injured in a car accident, and as I laid in bed in severe pain, I asked my husband, "Are you still here with me . . . to help me through this ordeal?"

As a result of my plea, I began to hear the sounds of my husband's boots during the night, walking up the attic stairs, and then the footsteps would continue overhead across the wooden attic floor, as though my husband patrolled throughout the house to protect me during my early recovery.

My sister, who along with her husband now lived with me, also heard the bewildering familiar sounds of my husband's boots coming from the empty space outside my closed bed-room door, while she watched TV alone, in the dinette area, during the dim hours of the night.

Additionally, very early one morning before dawn, while I recuperated in bed after having made my loving plea, I heard knocking on my bedroom wall that woke me. While sipping a cup of coffee in the dinette, my sister heard it too. Initially, the sound had frightened her, because she thought I died and the knocks might have been my way to let her know I had reached the other side.

After investigating this anomaly, by locating the area of the knocking, we both agreed the sound came from the interior wall which separated my bedroom from the living room. Since we each had an unobstructed view of both sides of the wall, we found no plausible explanation to justify the knocks, except to concur that they appeared to be paranormal in nature.

I have come to realize that it is during times of stressful anxiety when the spiritual phenomena becomes extremely active. In time, when my stress slowly subsides, the frequency of these paranormal activities lessen, or became subtler in intensity.

Those who believe that the essence of the soul can make contact from beyond our realm, should find comfort in the thought that our loved one's spirit lives on. And people who have had personal supernatural experiences of their own, should accept and cherish their own interpretation of the intent of the phenomena, without fear of being ridiculed.

It might be a person's lack of faith that causes them to reject the plausibility that God's omnificence created specific spiritual powers which are intended to be utilized by the essence of the soul after death, and that these abilities weren't expected to be developed by the mortal soul during our lifetime on earth.

Just because we don't have credible proof that spirits exist, or we question the ability of our life force to contact the living after death, one thing is for sure: *no one can say for certain that these probabilities are impossible.*

In support of my hypothesis of the spirit's existence and their capabilities after death, I have described just a few of the many spiritual anomalies I have encountered. These paranormal events have fortified my conviction that, "There is life after death. I have seen and felt its presence."

CHAPTER 46

How Difficult Could an Entry Level College Writing Course Be?

S lowly the pieces of my shattered life began to fall into place, but it wasn't without constant encouragement on my part. Daily, I forced myself to take the next step to overcome my grief. As the battle raged within, I decided a change in pace might be exactly what I needed.

Now, finding myself at a crossroad in my life, the time had come to decide if I should sign up for an Eastern Connecticut State University's writing course. Needless to say, I wanted to step out of my safe comfort zone and embark upon this important challenge, but I wondered if it might be more than I could handle, at a time in my life when my emotions erupted at the drop of a hat.

Therefore, the dilemma I now faced surrounded a doubt that troubled me. Did I feel emotionally competent to attend classes? Then again, if I did register, I may not be up to the challenge and could fail, but I was convinced that would be no worse than not trying at all.

Many times inspiration comes in the form of a thought we need to act upon, in order to accomplish a specific goal. Several people I spoke to since my husband's death, told me they admired my courage to tackle items on my bucket list, instead of just contemplating them. Some admitted, they two, under similar circumstances, had made a list, but had never pursued the difficult ones because it seemed like too much of an effort for them to attempt at the time.

It had been decades since I last attended school. I was out of touch with the demands a higher education placed upon its students and nervous about my ability to interact with strangers, especially a group of younger students who would be my peers.

Could I commit to the rigorous writing schedule a syllabus required? Was I up to the task or overestimating my capabilities at such a fragile time in my life? Should I break out of my shell and try to survive the perilous journey, like the newborn baby turtle hatchlings, who make their risky expedition to the sea, hoping to avoid being eaten by birds of prey?

Most importantly, I needed to stop concentrating upon the negativities of my situation before I talked myself out of taking the proper path. A common-sense approach would indicate that the only way to discover my true capabilities would be to register and try my best.

Of course, the fact I had enlisted the support of my brother-in-law helped make my decision a little easier. He, too, had toyed with the idea of writing for enjoyment during his retirement years, and agreed a refresher course would be a good place for us to start before either one of us delved any deeper into specific writing genres.

Taking all matters into consideration, my brother-in-law and I both registered for the spring semester at ECSU. Our joint venture helped thrust aside some of my insecurities, because now, I wouldn't be the only old person in class.

Thank goodness we made this choice, for we soon discovered our inexperience had nothing to do with our writing capabilities. Currently, we just didn't have a sound footing to build upon. The course was meant to teach research techniques, writing annotations, rhetorical analysis comprehension, criteria evaluations and different writing genres. One difficult writing assignment involved research for a scholarly paper. The 1,500-word project required a thesis, citations and most importantly, a scholarly argument based upon a non-obvious claim. The entire course turned out to be a formidable experience.

Even though I tried my best to convince my sister to join in on this stimulating adventure and take a class she might find interesting as well, she couldn't be coaxed into it. She responded to my invitation by pointing out that she never liked school when she had to go, and she found no pleasure in the thought of going back . . . just for fun.

Nevertheless, rather than staying at home while we labored away in class, my sister decided to keep us company on the drive to and from school. Therefore, for the three days a week our lectures took place, she leisurely sat and read at the University's library, enjoying a cup of coffee while she waited for our class to finish. Though she excelled in various other creative activities, she had no ambition to become a writer. She preferred relaxing, while thinking fondly of her husband and me, as we struggled through the course.

In addition to her entertaining company during the drive, she became our gourmet chef. Every day we met for class, she prepared tasty lunch dishes for all of us to enjoy once our lesson had concluded for the day. My brother-in-law and I became conditioned, like Pavlov's dogs, when we heard the buzzer signaling the end of our lecture, because we knew a delicious lunch awaited us.

Our first day of school was an education in and of itself. Although I had read the course syllabus and understood it to mean an introduction to basic writing, I never expected the intensity of the workload which followed. Within a very short period of time, I realized the course wasn't going to be an easy A.

Once I understood how difficult the curriculum would be, it was obvious I needed to put my book aside in order to keep my full concentration on my classwork. The course objective and time allotted for the completion of each assignment was far more difficult than I had anticipated. Or, more likely, I was just out of touch with the demands of school work.

Since my dream state was so active, I kept notes for my memoir, or I would have forgotten many important aspects of this critical period in my personal life

Little pieces of paper, scattered all over the dinette table, contained thoughts and ideas to be incorporated into my book when the moment was right.

Eventually, all these insightful notions were neatly tucked away into a folder, to be resurrected at an appropriate period of time when I would use them to describe the accurate portrayal of a life in need of healing.

The syllabus allotted a short two-week period to complete each writing assignment, with a four-week allocation for the difficult scholarly genre. At the end of each project, the professor expected each student to improve their strengths and weaknesses as a writer in rhetorical situations, multiple genres, as well as proper thesis development.

In the beginning, I found it difficult to interpret the proper techniques used to write diverse genres. I felt out of touch because the teaching methods were so different from what I remembered from a half-century ago.

Our professor insisted on critical thinking and was always available for one-on-one appointments to help those of us who got lost along the way. I took full advantage of this opportunity, because her assistance proved to be tremendously beneficial.

After completion of the course, I felt confident I had learned various new skills which involved detailed writing techniques and the use of in-depth thought processes. We were also taught how to acquire comprehensive research information through the use of proper references. So much work was bundled into so little time, but somehow we managed to get it all in.

I have provided a short synopsis of my Portfolio Reflection to present a brief summary of my before and after views of the course:

As I think back to the day I entered Room 231 of the Science Building at Eastern Connecticut State University for my first day of class in English 100, many thoughts ran through my

mind. *I wondered what writing abilities I had or could develop, and I hoped the course would be my litmus test to prove if I had talent, never expecting the demanding, grueling schedule of the writing assignments that followed.*

During my journey, I learned how to cultivate the utilization of academic concepts to develop my writing skills by incorporating critical thinking, proper research, appropriate evidence, organizational skills, and use of professional guidance in my work, which enabled me to evolve into a more efficient writer. I quickly learned there was so much more to writing than I had ever imagined. Most significantly, I wasn't disappointed in the progress I made throughout the semester. I strengthened many of my weaknesses, gained a solid passion for learning, and felt encouraged that I had been able to progressively tackle more difficult writing genres in a manner I would never have thought possible at the start.

I constantly strove to do my best, for the sheer enjoyment I obtained from the accomplishment of the task.

Undoubtably, the course was challenging. Psychologically speaking, even though I was still in the early stages of my grief, the difficult path I pursued enabled me to realize just how resilient I could be, so long as I was willing to take that first step forward in my journey of recovery.

And in answer to your question, yes . . . I did get an A.

CHAPTER 47

Have Faith and God Will Never Let You Down

In order to fill the lonely hours of the day since my husband's death, I took on most of the exterior household responsibilities my husband so skillfully managed while he was alive. The fall cleanup, from the leaves of the hundreds of oak trees which were scattered throughout our property, had been a daunting task. Thankfully, my brother-in-law provided me with a helping hand by running my Kubota tractor, while I handled the power vacuum which was attached to the suction hose of a leaf vacuum called a Cyclone Rake, that cleaned up the dried remnants of the once beautiful fall foliage. Although he suggested that he handle the heavy hose while I drove, I knew what portion of the grounds I wanted cleared, and I also felt he should save his strength for the worst portion of the job to come.

When it came time to empty the tightly packed 8-cubic feet of dirt and leaf remnants which had been sucked up into the body of the huge canvas vacuum bag of the Cyclone Rake, the most exhausting part of the job was to rake the material out of the bag by hand, once the vacuum's compartment was full.

To keep the property immaculate, the leaf clean-up work was a never-ending job, until the last of the mighty oak leaves

239

fell, and the remaining stragglers were chopped up by the lawn mower, when necessary.

Once the fall cleanup was completed, I had the snow removal responsibility to look forward to. Of course, I could hire someone to do this job, but I had more than a simple driveway which needed to be kept clear.

So far, the weather we had been enjoying this winter was on the mild side, but there was still eight weeks left till spring, and the weatherman said the time had come for a change in the forecast. The artic winds from the north suddenly decreased the milder temperatures we had been enjoying from the southerly flow, and now, the normal New England frigid winter conditions were on the horizon. Instead of the cold, chilling rain which had dominated our weather pattern so far this season, the forecast called for heavy snow . . . and I was not happy.

My husband was skilled at everything he did. Plowing the curvy driveway he designed was no exception. Except now, this responsibility fell upon me. I prayed I would get through the winter without having to deal with unmanageable snow, but today, my prayers would go unanswered.

Under normal circumstances, there would be no reason to clear the snow in the large area out back, where my husband's work garage was located. However, my house was for sale and needed to be meticulously maintained, in the event a showing took place. I had no doubt that potential customers would be interested in the workshop area, especially since it afforded such versatility in its use.

Besides, in the event I did sell my house and had to move before the end of winter, the movers would need access to all of the property. I also knew it was much easier to clear freshly fallen snow, than to try to move it once it hardens.

While my husband was still alive, at the time he was nearing the end of his battle against pancreatic cancer and fall was approaching, he worried how I would accomplish this daunting job once he was gone. Well aware of how difficult the winter snow cleanup would be, we discussed the option of hiring someone to do the work. Since the roads in our rural little corner of Southeastern CT could become treacherous during ice storms, and as these occurrences had become more frequent in recent years, my husband thought it best for me to be prepared and do the job myself. Whenever the temperatures were just right for ice or slush, it was difficult to drive up the steep hill, which provided access to our small subdivision, even though the main highway was located only a mile away. According to my husband's way of thinking, safety always came first. He felt I should be self-sufficient when it came to providing clear driveway passage for my car, as well as for oil truck or emergency vehicle access when necessary.

Therefore, after much thought, we decided the best solution would be to install a snow thrower attachment onto our enclosed heated farm tractor. This way, in his mind, I could handle clearing the snow in a warm and cozy environment. At the time, it seemed like a good idea.

We also owned a large ¾ ton, 4-wheel drive, diesel pickup truck, with a snow plow attachment. When I say large, that is an understatement. Unfortunately, for me, it had been years since I had even driven our cars. Now I was expected to drive this beast of a truck and plow snow at the same time!

My husband was so confident in my abilities, I didn't want him to be concerned about my insecurities. There was enough for him to worry about, dealing with his own illness. Besides, once he died, there was nothing he could do to help me.

Often I thought about the old saying, love is blind. I could tell by the way he spoke, he didn't see the age on my face, nor did he ever seem to question my ability. In his eyes, his wife was the Rock of Gibraltar; if only I felt the same.

Thank goodness I enjoyed keeping him company whenever he plowed snow. I was his shotgun rider and kept a look out for traffic, while he was preoccupied with the mechanics of plowing. The little bit of knowledge I acquired was a direct result of watching him. Ironically, at the time, neither of us ever realized I was being trained as his replacement.

Each time the snow cleanup was done, our reward was a nice hot cup of coffee at a local gas station. This was a treat we both enjoyed. He loved getting out on the road to check out the driving conditions. He never outgrew the adventure of testing his driving skills in all weather conditions.

During snow cleanup, as his unbeknownst apprentice, I learned early on that the first push out of the work garage was crucial. I remember one occasion, in particular, when my husband turned to me and said, "Wish me luck. I hope we can make it all the way down the driveway!"

That day, I closed my eyes and prayed he would succeed.

At that same time, I thought to myself, "In the event we got stuck, he would just get another piece of equipment and pull the truck out."

Unfortunately, I no longer had the security of knowing he would be there to take care of any problem which could arise. I had to deal with the frightening thought, I know how to drive the truck and the farm tractor, but if I get stuck, I have no idea how to dig myself out.

Now, in the midst of winter, my luck had finally run out. The first plowable snow since my husband's death was underway. But instead of all snow, the temperatures were just right and ice was now accumulating on top of the heavy snow. Throughout the night, as the snow deepened, and I heard ice pinging against the window panes in my bedroom, I became extremely anxious. I knew the situation wasn't good, especially, since I was on my own to tackle the intimidating job ahead of me.

Once morning arrived, it was still snowing. Adding to my concerns, the snow-covered roads were coated with a sheet of ice that had made them impassable. My sister and her husband weren't living with me as of yet, so they wouldn't be able to drive to my house until the following day to help clear the snow and ice from the walks, patios and pathways, as they had promised my husband they would do before he died.

Since I was completely unfamiliar with the operation of the new snow thrower, and this would be my maiden voyage, I waited until the storm had finally stopped before I started to begin my cleanup, around noon.

The snow was too deep and heavy to shovel, with the added weight of the icy rain on top. Because I didn't know how to use the hand operated snow blower my husband always used to clear the 600-foot path to the work garage where the tractor was kept, I had no option but to trudge through the deep snow.

As I looked around at the monumental task in front of me, I was overwhelmed. I knew it was going to be difficult, but I was surprised by the emotional impact I felt when I entered my husband's work garage without him by my side.

Choking back tears, I climbed into the tractor to start it. I had to remember to heat up the glow plug, pre-heat the engine and let it idle before I could engage the snow thrower.

My instructions were written down because I am not mechanically inclined, and there was no one else around to help if I couldn't remember. I always said, "My memory is good; it is just short." After I opened the large overhead garage door, I set the diverter for proper ground clearance and turned the snow thrower switch on. Unsure of myself, I slowly made my first pathway into the deep snow.

The minute I cleaned a large enough area behind the garage to operate from, I climbed out of the tractor and went back inside to close the overhead door, in order to keep the heat inside and secure the building. Now, I had to walk out the side door, through mounds of snow, in order to get back into the tractor. My hopes of an easy cleanup didn't materialize, as I struggled to figure out where I could put all of the newly fallen snow.

Although my husband had made it look easy, I immediately realized it wasn't. Instead, it took me hours of clearing, until I finally reached the main house garage area. To make matters worse, it began to snow again, and there was still at least another 800 feet to clear before I reached the road at the end of my driveway.

The salesman who sold me the snow thrower attachment, after my husband's death, had warned me that if the ground wasn't frozen on the sides of the asphalt driveway, or in the gravel area out back, I must keep the diverter which collected the snow a minimum of 3-4 inches off the ground. So far this season, the winter temperatures had remained warm enough to prevent the normal winter ground freeze, even though it was already February. Therefore, I tried hard to follow this advice, since it was crucial for me to maintain a proper elevation in order to prevent the soft dirt from entering the chute and clogging it.

This was easier said than done. Every time I put the tractor into reverse in order to back up, I had to maneuver the lever to lift and adjust the bucket, or else I would end up redistributing the snow on the ground I had just cleared. Once I was ready to push forward, to start clearing the snow again, I had to remember to put the bucket back down and realign the ground clearance before I re-engaged the blower. Since this was all new to me, I was constantly moving levers back and forth, and it was very easy to forget to set the proper elevation. Fortunately, so far, all had gone well.

Only now, it was already 9 p.m. and I was really tired. I had been clearing snow for the past nine hours. Although I seemed to be making headway, suddenly I hit an unfrozen portion of the lawn on the right side of the main house driveway. Immediately, the shoot packed with dirt and stopped working, so I shut the tractor down in order to inspect the damage.

In order to assess the situation, I got out of the tractor and stood outside in the darkness. I felt cold while the snow, which had just recently restarted, gently fell upon me.

The paved portion of the driveway in front of the main house garage area, which I had just recently cleared, was now full of a mixture of snow, dirt and ice, which had blown out of the shoot before it stopped working. If I didn't find a way to clean it up, with the current temperatures and moisture in the air, it would freeze overnight, and I wouldn't be able to back my car out of the garage if I needed to use it the next day. I was frustrated and felt defeated, but told myself, I wouldn't cry. Instead, I looked up toward Heaven to ask my husband for help.

Suddenly, subconsciously, I heard my husband's encouraging words, "Take the tractor down back to the work garage that is heated. Turn on the garage lights, clean out the chute, and then get back outside to finish the job!"

I couldn't help but smile at the inspirational intervention I had received. So, I did exactly what I was told to do.

Soon, the machine was up and running. I took a shovel from the garage and put it in the cab. When I reached the spot where the tractor went down, I took one shovel of the dirt and snow mixture at a time, until I cleaned up the mess and only white snow remained. In time, I managed to clear the rest of the turn-around area and began to tackle the remainder of the driveway. I was on the home stretch at last!

As I got closer to the road, I saw a large tree limb had fallen across the driveway, which obstructed my path. I now wondered how many more problems I would have to tackle before the night was over.

If I didn't push it out of the way, I would be blocked in until morning, when I could call for help. Uncertain if the tractor had enough power and stability on the icy driveway, I needed to figure out how to tackle this obstacle and prevent the tractor from losing traction on the slippery ground. I decided it would be sensible to use the side of the tractor bucket to operate like a plow and push the limb far enough off the asphalt in order to clear the driveway of the debris. My first attempt was successful and enabled me to finish clearing the rest of the snow off the driveway, all the way up to the town road.

By now it was late into the night and the clouds were starting to break. I could see some stars twinkling in the unobstructed portions of the sky. When I looked around at the beauty of the moonlight glistening off the crystalizing ice and snow, which held down all the tree limbs now bent down to the ground by the weight of the accumulation, the scenery was breathtaking and inspiring.

I remember thinking how magnificent our Heavenly Father is to have created such beauty. Yearningly, I wished my husband could have been physically present, instead of spiritually, to enjoy the serenity of the night.

Unquestionably, I felt both God's and my husband's presence with me that night, as I was guided and provided strength during my weakness.

While discussing my experiences of tackling difficult jobs on my own with friends and new acquaintances, I could tell when certain individuals understood what I had gone through. Although my narrative usually included a comedic monologue of the events, those who recently lost a spouse or dear family member would say that they had also felt their departed loved ones were there to help them when they needed it most.

The touching responses I usually received made me realize how important it was for me to pass on all the inspirational events I had been blessed to experience.

It is so important to realize we are never alone, even in our darkest hour. Although our inner strength is constant, at times we need to ask for help, and it may come in unsuspecting ways.

During the next storm, I decided to use the snow plow. To my surprise, it was easier to operate. Because the next storm's accumulation wasn't too deep, I managed to plow the driveway without disturbing the unfrozen ground.

Since this was the first time I drove the truck out of the garage with the plow on it, when I finished clearing the snow, it took me four tries to back through the narrow garage door opening to park the truck inside, until I needed to plow again. Due to the size of the vehicle, I was stressed while maneuvering through the tight space, but I pictured my husband watching me from up above. I was amused and smiled as I spoke these words to my husband, "I know you are looking down at me laughing, but I am trying my best!"

Always remember, never give up. It is amazing how strong we can be in times of adversity. While I knew I could call upon others for help, I discovered I was able to accomplish many difficult chores on my own.

What I am trying to say is, although life is difficult, no one can complete our journey for us. Unless we try to help ourselves, we will never complete the jobs that bring us the satisfaction of knowing we can survive the hurdles placed before us, which ultimately make us stronger. Have faith in God's inspiration. He will never let you down.

CHAPTER 48

Positive Energy

I discovered the Monsignor was correct when he administered the services of the Last Rites for my husband on the
morning of his death, and expressed his opinion that some
people will experience spiritual activity in their lives after the
loss of a loved one. Although he said these events would
lessen in time, apparently not enough time had passed for
me, especially since my experiences were manifesting by
leaps and bounds.

Thank goodness the apparition and bed movements had
stopped, but the flickering lights and computer interference
were still common events. To a certain degree, I was amused
by the various incidents I experienced. In a way, I enjoyed
the cat and mouse game my husband and I shared, since
it provided a small degree of happiness during a period of
incredible grief.

I accepted every unexplained episode as a means to
help me deal with my husband's loss, since each time they
occurred, they represented a positive affirmation that his
spirit lived on. Surely, appreciating this form of phenomena
as a band aid to help heal a portion of one's grief may not
be the answer for everyone. Personally, I found joy in each
experience. At this stage in my grief, I still needed this type
of validation, which was probably the reason the incidents
continued to occur.

Although I am certain there are many people who believe in a spirit's ability to contact the living, it isn't my goal to convince those who don't that they should embrace this concept. Instead, it is my intention to help you heal, by discovering the little things in life which can make you feel better about your situation.

Some forms of grief relief may be achieved by reading self-help books; making new friends, in addition to valuing the old ones who still keep in touch; as well as finding new interests or hobbies. The repetition of familiar activities you previously shared with your loved one may sometimes result in the resurrection of your grief. I noticed that each new activity I successfully accomplished provided me with a feeling of satisfaction for a job well done. Therefore, you may discover, the pursuit of new activities may lessen your feeling of loss by creating cheerful memories to contemplate. These small changes may help you find a bit of happiness, where currently only sorrow exists.

Furthermore, in addition to following my new motivation to write, I found peace in my nightly prayer ritual because the goal in my life had changed. When I realized my path had become a spiritual objective, rather than a desire for earthly endeavors, I was pleasantly surprised how simple my life became.

Because family circumstances or personal issues you encounter at the time of the death of your loved one may be different from mine, your choices may differ widely from mine. My pursuit for inner peace was my guide. Of course, I had no children to raise or work schedules to maintain, which made my choices unique to my situation. Just bear in mind that the direction you choose to follow, at this difficult juncture, should provide some form of happiness and fulfillment to slowly replace your grief.

As a result of the spiritual course I chose, inspiration crossed my path one night, which triggered a fascinating otherworldly event to occur. Instead of using the rosary I had purchased at the little religious shop in Colchester during my husband's illness, I felt compelled to retrieve the Medjugorje

Rosary from the special place where it was stored for safe-keeping. Then, with my husband's rosary in hand, I sat down at the dinette table to pray. Once I held the beads between my fingers, I felt as though his treasured gift continued to provide comfort, only now, I was the recipient of its encouragement. Soon I was deep in prayer, engrossed in the reflection of one of the mysteries. Before I knew it, I had completed the five decades of the rosary, and it was time for bed.

Before retiring for the evening, I walked into my front foyer to confirm that the front door was locked, when I faintly heard the tolling of a clock. The chiming gave me the impression the sound came from upstairs. As I climbed the staircase, I recognized the ringing of the old heirloom clock we kept in my daughter's now vacant bedroom. It sounded a total of nine times, but by the time I entered the room, the striking had stopped. I walked over and looked to see if the clock was running, but it was not.

This clock is an old wooden Westinghouse Tambour mantel clock, that my husband and I inherited many years ago after my husband's father had died. It was a wedding gift his parents had received, dating back to the 1930's. Although the clock hadn't worked for over 20 years, and had no monetary value, it had a strong sentimental significance, which was the main reason we treasured it.

Since there was no other clock upstairs, the chiming must have come from this particular clock, and the sound brought back enjoyable memories of my husband and his parents. A pleasurable warm feeling came over me, and I credited my first time use of the Medjugorje Rosary to be the cause of this fascinating event. Undaunted by the experience, I went on to check and make sure the rest of the house was secure before I got ready for bed.

Exhausted from working on the computer all day, once I settled into bed, I quickly fell asleep. I can't say how long it took before I awoke to the vision of two hands, slender and delicate in design, reaching for my face . . . but then again, I could have woken up from a dream as well. The hands appeared to be close together and were surrounded by light.

They almost touched me, as though my chin was about to be cupped in a tender embrace. The clarity of the image was absolute, and I was in awe of the vision's beauty, but as I looked on, the visualization quickly disappeared.

Instead of feeling afraid, I felt reverence. The image reminded me of pictures I had seen of the Blessed Virgin Mary's outstretched hands, offering Her children a message of love and hope.

Three nights later, I had a beautiful dream. I saw tall thin trees, bare of limbs all the way up, until I viewed the treetops. At the skyline, the trees were capped with delicate green leaves, in a round ball shape design, and warm summer breezes ruffled the leaves within.

There were golden rays of sunlight, which covered the whole sky and gleamed down through the leaves of the multitude of trees. As I followed the rays down to the ground, I felt as though I was in paradise enjoying a privileged view from a hilltop.

I watched as men and women strolled along a meadow, with books in their arms. They were dressed in magnificently colored, long brocade garments, reminiscent of old Grecian attire. The outfits consisted of bold purples, reds, yellows, and greens, which dazzle the human eye, because the shades of color were beyond description in their intensity.

The entire scene created an image of serenity, which I longed to be a part of, but upon awakening, I understood that I was not. I felt no sadness by this realization, because I had been encouraged by the thought that such tranquility may exist, even if only in my imagination.

I presumed that all three events, the clock, the image of the hands, and the dream, were subtle messages of inspiration sent to encourage me, and give me hope.

When I relay these experiences, I hope to illustrate how our thoughts and dreams can turn our sadness into comfort. If you are willing to accept even the slightest bit of the inspiration you receive, as an invitation to take advantage of the abundance of positive energy which surrounds you, the healing of your grief will follow.

CHAPTER 49

Why Do We Have to Suffer? The Answer Was Simple

Winter was slowly turning into spring, and the buds were starting to show their red tint in the trees, though I wasn't looking forward to a reminder that it was during this time last year when my husband's illness surfaced and changed my life forever.

Although I had been able to find direction in my life, that didn't mean I found an escape from the pain and sorrow I experienced since my husband's death. Every day I prayed to God for strength, but recently, I had been asking for a sign to let me know he was okay.

One morning, after showering and dressing, I walked across the bedroom to shut off the TV before heading to the kitchen to start my day with a hot cup of coffee. When I picked up the remote from my night stand, out of the right corner of my eye, I noticed something unusual on my husband's side of the bed. Upon closer inspection, it turned out to be a penny. Since I don't sit or dress on his side of the bed, I wouldn't expect to find a coin on my freshly made bed. So, I attributed the penny as a message from heaven that all was well.

I needed this reassurance because a drastic change was taking place in my life. It was time to sell my house and make the difficult choices that coincide with this type of event. I hated the thought of moving, especially since this necessitated the liquidation of many of the items my husband and I had purchased throughout our lives together. Obviously, when I downsized to a smaller home, I wouldn't have enough space to fit everything. The elimination of years of loving memories would be a struggle I must contend with, especially since the thought of disposing of my husband's belongings hurt beyond belief.

As I contemplated my current situation, I asked myself, "Are things in my life going well?" My answer, "Maybe not as good as I hoped," pretty much summed it up.

I cried when it came time to sell my husband's personal tools and clean out his work garage in preparation for the anticipated sale of our home. Every tool I touched reminded me of how hard my husband worked throughout his life. I recalled so many occasions when I sat with him, to keep him company, while he tinkered in his shop on a list of repairs which never seemed to end.

The hardest thing I had to face was disposing of his clothes. It didn't make sense to keep them in our closet when there were people who could use them. Actually, it took a while before I separated the few jackets, shirts and pants I simply couldn't give away, in order to dispose of the rest. Often, I ran my fingers over his remaining clothes, which still hang in my closet.

If I didn't have to move, I wouldn't have undertaken any of these projects so quickly, if at all. Therefore, I tackled one job at a time, instead of placing myself in a more difficult situation where I would have to get rid of the unusable items when I sold my home. Using common sense, I could carefully choose special mementos I wanted to keep, so I wouldn't be stressed out during the moving process by having to deal with this difficult task all at one time.

Up until this point, I felt like I was doing better. Unfortunately, the anticipated move and downsizing was constantly reminding me of my loss, which now disrupted my life all over again. It was during this sad process when I asked God, "Why do we have to suffer like this?"

The answer I received was simple, "Life is not easy, but you chose your life and now you must complete it, as it was intended."

Enlightened by this statement, I found contentment in its simplicity. This explanation helped me understand that my husband's death was not intended to inflict pain or punishment upon me. His death represented the completion of his journey, in the hopes he had learned the lessons he came to earth to ascertain.

During the portion of my lifespan that I shared with my husband, our lives interacted in a positive way with many people on earth. Upon his death, I realized there must still be instances where my help was needed before I could rest.

This revelation didn't suddenly change my world and make everything better. However, it did help me understand I wasn't traveling my path alone. I was constantly being helped through God's intervention, as well as human interaction, when I couldn't make it on my own. Now it was up to me to return the favor to others who are in need.

My faith in God, along with the support I received from so many loving people after my husband's death, allowed me to accept the inevitable and move on. Throughout my journey, there is one thing I have learned for certain, "Life is not easy, but I chose my life (in Heaven) and now I must complete it, as it was intended."

CHAPTER 50

I Found Comfort in
Unusual Places

Acceptance of the fact my life was now being experienced as an I, and not as a we, was finally hitting home. For most of my life, many of the important decisions my husband and I made were joint ones. It definitely wasn't easy to reprogram my brain to think independently.

Since I slowly started to make my own decisions without second guessing myself every step of the way, I concluded my healing process was progressing, and I was on the mend.

I now assumed that I might possibly have reached an important turning point in my life, because every so often, I actually found myself smiling and enjoying a little bit of happiness. This might be due to the fact that I now concentrated on the good times my husband and I enjoyed together, instead of dwelling upon the pain associated with his loss.

Whenever possible, I found it helpful to put a humorous spin on a negative situation. For example, the first time I had difficulty parking my husband's plow truck in the work garage, instead of getting angry, I conceptually joked with my husband about my lack of coordination. I knew, if my husband were alive, we would have laughed together, considering how comical it must have looked to watch me back up his truck through such a confined space.

Surprisingly, I also found comfort in the knowledge I wasn't alone in life's sorrows. I'm not saying I found happiness knowing others grieved due to their loss. The exact opposite was true. I now felt extreme compassion for individuals who suffered similar fates, because until you have experienced such a devastating event, it is impossible to understand the damaging effects it has upon the survivor.

Once I put into perspective the fact that the pain I endured, as a result of my loss, is suffered universally by all, and I rationalized the common sense notion that I wasn't personally chosen to be the intended object of an assault upon my happiness by humanity because it was my husband's time to die, I discovered my acceptance of the fact that death is an unavoidable casualty of life was an important step in my recovery.

And, although I have found comfort in unusual places, I realize I will never completely get over my loss, but I will learn to live within its boundaries.

CHAPTER 51

Cherished Moments

As I continue on with my life, I realize how important it is to remember the happy times, the cherished moments I shared with my husband. All too often, I found it was too easy to drift toward the negativities in my life . . . the *what if's* and the *why me* scenarios. These thoughts served no useful purpose, except to draw out the emotional sadness I was trying to overcome.

I found comfort in the knowledge that I wasn't alone when it came to survivor's sorrow, as odd as this statement may seem, because I realized that people who have traveled this path understand the desolation and difficulties survivors face, and therefore have a better understanding of how grief can consume their life. Interestingly enough, I discovered that friendship bonds develop quickly between survivors who have suffered a similar loss.

A death is a death, is a death . . . no matter whether it resulted from years of illness, an instantaneous accident, murder or suicide. Whatever catastrophic event caused the end of our loved one's existence, the anguish and chaos that affects the life of the survivor(s) is overwhelming.

If I were to survive and wanted to thrive, I realized I needed to learn how to cope. That was the hard part . . . and is still a work in progress.

There are many facets of grief one has to deal with. For some, in addition to the sadness, guilt becomes a factor.

In my case, my husband had to have known he was experiencing stomach distress, but he didn't share this information with me. There were tests he could have taken, which were available through his yearly health checkups, but he chose not to have them performed; most likely, because he didn't want to know the results.

The decision was his to make, but I must profess, I am no better when it comes to my own health issues.

Obviously I didn't want my husband to die, and I wish I had talked him into performing standardized medical tests when his physician suggested them, but many of us are either too busy, or really don't want to know if there is a problem affecting our health. So, like my husband, people will procrastinate, sometimes, until it is too late.

We can blame ourselves from sunup to sundown because we could have been more proactive in our efforts, but holding ourselves accountable will not change the outcome. Therefore, the acceptance of a non-guilt position is a good place to start when we travel through our journey of grief.

Despite the fact that the medical field has made much progress in finding cures for so many illnesses, it still isn't an exact science. Some seemingly innocent maladies, which should be easily cured, can turn out to be deadly.

Let's assume this is where the God factor comes into play. If it is God's will, and the time has come for a person to die, the outcome will most likely still be the same, even if all the facts are known and addressed during the patient's treatment period. The same holds true for accidents. It is an unfortunate part of life, because we live in a world where we simply don't have control over these types of events.

Do yourself a favor and try not to take on the blame for a loved one's passing. I can attest to the fact that there is more than enough burden to carry just surviving the death.

So instead, I chose to put a positive spin on the course of events which led to my husband's demise. Since he suffered from Parkinson's disease, which had no cure, I believe God was kind in allowing my husband to die sooner, rather than later. This way, he was spared suffering through worsening Parkinson's symptoms, which under his current circumstances had already caused him much distress.

When the time came to accept the role of caregiver as part of my life's journey, I would be lying if I said it was easy. Yet, because I loved him so much, I wouldn't want my husband to have traveled his difficult journey alone. Instead of being angry at God for setting off the events in my husband's life which caused me to become the survivor in our relationship, I was grateful to Him. That is because it gave me the opportunity to provide for his physical as well as his emotional needs along his arduous journey. In truth, I believe I benefited more from this experience than he did, because one of love's greatest gifts is to be able to share the sorrow associated with helping a loved one through their passage to death.

Another difficult element some survivors must deal with is death by suicide, with its many unanswered questions. The thought *why did you do this* is not easy to live with and can cause additional pain to those left behind. Although financial burdens or sadness may sometimes be the simplest explanation, medication and/or drugs can also be to blame.

Had my husband lived, I often worried about the possible negative side effects the elevation of his Parkinson's medication, as a result of the progression of his disease, might have caused. My research suggested Parkinson's medication, and often prescribed antidepressants, have resulted in veteran deaths by suicide as a result of their treatment. Unfortunately, this is the case in many degenerative diseases, and since there is no alternative treatment available, many patients are left with limited options.

Though I don't have any explanation for the actual mental instability which causes a person to commit suicide, I pray the survivor accepts the supposition that in some situations a chemical imbalance in the brain, due to certain medications, may have been the cause.

Regardless of the dreadful anxiety a person may have suffered through, which might possibly have caused them to take such a drastic measure as suicide, the survivor needs to realize that the individual person is the one responsible for their own death and no one else! Many of us face earth-shattering events which lure us into despondency, but most people don't give up on life.

If you need someone to blame, let God take on the responsibility for the cause of an untimely death. Then, as the survivor(s), you can hopefully get on with your life without feeling guilty. After all, death is a spiritual matter between the deceased and the Lord. You don't have to justify the reason the event took place in order to heal. Most often, the need to know the reason that actually triggered the suicide has more to do with an elimination of the blame a survivor carries for an incident they didn't cause. The fact that you are suffering the emotional loss of your loved one causes more than enough pain in your life. Don't take on the extra burden of undeserved guilt.

When the time came to consider sheltering myself from the lonely life I would soon face once my husband died, I never dwelt on the anticipation of his death while he was still alive. I didn't want to predict how I would go on with my life without him. Therefore, I concentrated upon living life during the dwindling hours we spent together, prior to his death, instead of living in fear of his death.

Actually, the end of his life was a reality I really hadn't accepted until the moment of truth, when his soul no longer existed inside his body, and God had received his spirit.

Once he passed on, my life came to a standstill. The morning I woke up to find my husband had died, although he didn't leave me by choice, I still felt abandoned. I fell apart, like the broken pieces of a ceramic figurine which had been shattered in a fall from its resting place. I was broken and didn't know how to put the pieces of my life back together again. I didn't even know where to start.

Now that my husband's pain was finally over, the time had come for me to find relief for my own agony, which wouldn't be a quick or easy fix.

After the funeral, I allowed myself the luxury to feel sorry for myself. I took as much time as I needed to be isolated from family and friends, until I was ready to rejoin society again. More importantly, I gave myself permission to cry, at the drop of a hat, or at a moment's notice, without regard to what anyone else might have thought. This was my gift to me.

Then, slowly, a path riddled with tears of sadness began to emerge. I found the broken pieces weren't as bad as I thought, and the glue I used to repair my broken heart was my interaction with family and friends who reached out to help me; those special people who didn't give up on me when I was unable to move forward. They waited, patiently, always extending a helping hand, until I was ready to come out of my cocoon and gradually transform into a butterfly with wings of my own.

In return, I promised myself that I would pass forward their kindnesses. Throughout my book, I have provided lessons I have learned, which helped me survive the pain and sorrow grief so generously bestowed upon me. Survivors, like me, who have suffered such a loss, need to shout out that there is a light at the end of the tunnel!

Even though I believe time does heal most wounds, unfortunately, it may never totally eradicate them. In fact, this is why I keep my good memories to fall back upon, during the times I stumble and fall . . . the occasions when I still need comfort from my grief.

I now want to share a beautiful dream which transpired almost a year after my husband's death; one of the magical experiences I enjoy, which helps me find contentment in the most unusual places. Whether encouragement comes from life experiences, spiritual solicitations, or are dream induced, my recollection of pleasant memories is sometimes enough to get me though those spontaneous bouts of sadness which occur.

The Domed Room

While I sat next to my husband in our convertible, we magically floated along a tree lined dirt road. As we approached a clearing, a large, wooden structure appeared on the right side of a freshly cut pasture of green grass. The vision was so alluring, I could almost smell the cuttings.

Outside of the building, I watched as people moseyed along, admiring the beautiful plants, shrubs and flowers which lined the manicured, open-aired portion of the nursery.

Once we reached the building, my husband and I walked through an unpretentious doorway entrance and emerged in a large domed room, ablaze with bright, brilliant illumination from the ceiling above. The room flourished with 10-foot-tall stately trees, featuring protruding delicate, thin branches, adorned with shimmering gold and silver flowers, resembling a peonies floral design.

I felt like I was in heaven and recalled being overcome with a sense of awe because of the majestic beauty I saw. The oversized blooms were approximately 24" in diameter, and there were multiple flowers at the end of each branch. The pedals glistened and flickered in the sunlight, which radiated from the dome above, upon the stunning display of God's exquisite elegance.

As we began to walk down a dirt lane, which divided the orchard in half, I suddenly realized that only sparkling golden flowers were flourishing on my right side, while dazzling silver ones adorned my left. It was at this moment that I realized these trees were special, and they were not for sale. I believed the only purpose for their existence was to relish their beauty, because the flowers on earth did not sparkle and were neither silver nor gold.

Suddenly, I found myself alone outside, looking at flowering trees that were for sale. They were similar in structure, only smaller. The flowering peonies, which grew on these plants, were closer to 10 inches in diameter, and the trees were approximately four feet in height.

After contemplating my options, I noticed that each tree contained approximately four branches, and each branch bloomed with blossoms consisting of a distinct, brilliant color. The shades ranged from white to dazzling crimson rose, along with radiant tones of coral, peach and salmon. Their essence of beauty was beyond comparison to the colors I have seen on earth.

When I finally picked up and held the perfect multicolored flowering plant that I had decided to buy, I woke up.

While absentmindedly driving along the back roads during the following morning, I found myself daydreaming. As I thought about my previous night's dream, contemplating my husband's presence in the mystical garden paradise with its heavenly undertones, I suddenly discovered that I had taken a wrong turn and found myself driving past the cemetery. And so, my enchanted dream was reason enough for me to turn in for a visit.

My mind was in a good place, cheered on by delightful thoughts, until I reached his gravesite and realized that the summer floral arrangement I had made for him was missing. Since a groundskeeper was working in the vicinity, I decided to look around in a few of the refuse receptacles situated nearby, to see if the flowers had mistakenly been discarded, but they were nowhere to be found. Suddenly my optimistic attitude turned to thoughts of sadness instead, and I became determined to replace the flowers before the end of the day.

When I entered the store where I usually bought the individual dried flowers, I began to question if my dream had been a premonition, because I was surprised to see multiple peonies in colors similar to those glorified in my dream. This could have been a coincidence, or might it possibly have been a sign? In either case, I would like to believe that my husband had reached out to me to let me know I was on his mind.

Accept happiness wherever you can find it. The cherished moments I enjoy, which helps me achieve a calmness which seems to lighten the load my own grief has laid upon me, is a key you might use to unlock the pain lodged within your own heart. Hopefully, my techniques might enable you to find tranquility in your life once more.

How we deal with grief is a very personal matter. There is no right or wrong way to get through your anguish, no timetable or magic wand to make things instantly better. You must face your sorrow and determine what procedures or behavioral changes you can incorporate in your life that will improve your outlook. When you discover what simple steps you can take to create happiness, make sure to utilize these measures as a tool to reconstruct your life.

Most importantly, understand that it is not necessary to travel your journey alone. If you need help, reach out to your family, friends, support groups, or your church. There are many people who care and are willing to help, even though, at the moment, you may feel abandoned and alone.

The source of emotional pain we each experience may be as varied as the ripples in a stream, which are caused by the shallow water rushing over pebbles that became rounded through erosion over centuries of time. Just like the jagged stones smooth in their environment, you too can heal, by creating positive repetitive actions which are intended to offset the sad event that has taken over your life.

Although the death of a loved one makes life's struggle even more difficult to endure, once you get through the worst day, which is always the day before today, you need only take one tiny step at a time.

So as you deal with death as part of your journey in life, consider this thought: Life is a delicate balance between sorrow and joy.

Therefore, with love in my heart, I want to wish you success on your journey. May you find the inner peace you seek, and may God Bless you along your way.

Citations

Roure, Lucien. "Visions and Apparitions." The Catholic Encyclopedia. Vol. 15. New York: Robert Appleton Company, 1912. 18 Sept. 2016 http://www.newadvent.org/cathen/15477a.htm

Asaff, Beth. "The Different Colors of Ghost Orbs and Their Meanings" http://paranormal.lovetoknow.com (accessed December 30, 2017 @ 2:54 pm)

Painter, Sally "Spirit Orb Size and Color" http://paranormal.lovetoknow.com (accessed December 30, 2017 @ 2:54 pm)

Helmenstine, Anne Marie, Ph.D. "Why Are Light and Heat Not Matter?" ThoughtCo. https://www.thoughtco.com/light-and-heat-not-matter-608352 (accessed January 1, 2018).

Alexander, Eben. Proof of Heaven: A Neurosurgeon's Journey into the Afterlife. New York: Simon & Schuster Paperbacks, 2012. Print.

Tooley, Lawrence E. I Saw Heaven! A Remarkable Visit to the Spirit World. Bountiful, Utah: Horizon Publishers, ©1997.

Newton, Michael. Destiny of Souls: New Case Studies of Life between Lives. St. Paul, MN: Llewellyn Publications, 2000. Print.

Eaton, Barry. Afterlife: Uncovering the Secrets of Life After Death. New York: Jeremy P. Tarcher/Penguin, a member of Penguin Group (USA), 2013.

Guggenheim, Bill, and Judy Guggenheim. Hello From Heaven. Bantam Hardcover edition New York: Bantam books, 1996. Print.